The Guyot Geographical Reader and Primer

You are holding a reproduction of an original work that is in the public domain in the United States of America, and possibly other countries. You may freely copy and distribute this work as no entity (individual or corporate) has a copyright on the body of the work. This book may contain prior copyright references, and library stamps (as most of these works were scanned from library copies). These have been scanned and retained as part of the historical artifact.

This book may have occasional imperfections such as missing or blurred pages, poor pictures, errant marks, etc. that were either part of the original artifact, or were introduced by the scanning process. We believe this work is culturally important, and despite the imperfections, have elected to bring it back into print as part of our continuing commitment to the preservation of printed works worldwide. We appreciate your understanding of the imperfections in the preservation process, and hope you enjoy this valuable book.

THE GUYOT

GEOGRAPHICAL READER AND PRIMER

A SERIES OF JOURNEYS ROUND THE WORLD

BY

MARY HOWE SMITH PRATT

———o⦂⊙⦂o———

NEW YORK ∴ CINCINNATI ∴ CHICAGO
AMERICAN BOOK COMPANY

Copyright, 1882, by
CHARLES SCRIBNER'S SONS.

Copyright, 1898, by
AMERICAN BOOK COMPANY.

GEOG. READ. & PRIM.
W. P. 10

PREFACE

GUYOT'S INTRODUCTION has been pronounced by competent authorities to be the best of school reading books. This judgment has led the publishers to present this work in a form more attractive and available for class-room uses. The occasion has been improved to revise it thoroughly, and by changes, additions, and omissions to give it a completeness such as is indicated by its new name.

The value of such a Reader is obvious. The material presented is interesting and useful as matter of knowledge; its familiar and colloquial style awakens interest in the subject, creates easy and natural tones of expression, and leaves a lasting impression on the mind.

In order to complete its usefulness as a class book, the leading geographical facts are gathered up and presented in Part II. as a Primer of Lessons. This part is a brief outline of geography for beginners; noticing the *location* and *commercial and political* character of the countries, the *nature* of which, with much of their *life,* has been given in Part I. The form of these lessons, and their intimate connection with the readings, are such as to make mere repetition of words without thoughts altogether impossible.

THE GUYOT GEOGRAPHICAL READER AND PRIMER is believed to embody, both in the choice of material for its grade and in the mode of treatment, the best results of thought and experience on the part of the most earnest and practical educators.

CONTENTS.

Part I.

	PAGE
INTRODUCTION	1
NORTH AMERICA.	
UNITED STATES.	
The Atlantic Plain	4
The Appalachian Mountains	14
The Central Plain	20
The Mississippi	23
The Hudson	37
The Great Lakes and the St. Lawrence	46
Lake Champlain and Adirondacks	56
New England	59
Rocky Mountain Country	63
The Table-land	66
California	70
In the Northwest	75
NORTHERN LANDS	78
SOUTHERN LANDS	82
SOUTH AMERICA.	
AMAZON AND SILVAS	89
ANDES	97
PLAINS OF THE ORINOCO	102
PLAINS OF THE LA PLATA	105
ATLANTIC OCEAN	108
EUROPE.	
BRITISH ISLES	113
ATLANTIC COAST COUNTRIES	122
SOUTHWESTERN PENINSULAS	135
CENTRAL AND SOUTHEASTERN EUROPE	145
RUSSIA	158
AFRICA	160
ASIA	167
AUSTRALIA	180
PACIFIC OCEAN	182
CONCLUSION (Poem)	184

CONTENTS.

Part II.

	PAGE
INTRODUCTORY LESSONS	187
NORTH AMERICA.	
UNITED STATES.	
General Lessons	207
New England	215
Middle States	220
Southern States	224
Central States	230
Pacific States	234
DOMINION OF CANADA	240
MEXICO, CENTRAL AMERICA, AND WEST INDIES	241
SOUTH AMERICA.	
COUNTRIES OF THE PLAINS	244
COUNTRIES OF THE ANDES	246
EXAMINATION ON WESTERN HEMISPHERE	248
EUROPE.	
THE CONTINENT	250
BRITISH ISLES	251
FRANCE, BELGIUM, AND THE NETHERLANDS	254
THE NORTH COUNTRIES	255
MEDITERRANEAN COUNTRIES (SUNNY LANDS)	257
SWITZERLAND AND GERMANY	259
AUSTRIA-HUNGARY	261
RUSSIA AND ROUMANIA	264
AFRICA.	
NORTHERN AFRICA	268
MIDDLE AND SOUTHERN AFRICA	269
ASIA.	
NORTHERN AND WESTERN ASIA	272
THE INDIES	273
CHINESE AND JAPANESE EMPIRES	275
AUSTRALIA	278
EXAMINATION ON EASTERN HEMISPHERE	280
TABLES FOR REFERENCE	281

LIST OF MAPS.

		PAGES
1.	HEMISPHERES (double page)	194, 195
2.	UNITED STATES (double page)	212, 213
3.	NEW ENGLAND STATES	219
4.	MIDDLE STATES	225
5.	SOUTHERN STATES	229
6.	CENTRAL STATES	235
7.	PACIFIC STATES	239
8.	NORTH AMERICA	243
9.	SOUTH AMERICA	249
10.	BRITISH ISLES	253
11.	CENTRAL EUROPE	263
12.	EUROPE	267
13.	AFRICA	271
14.	ASIA	277

GEOGRAPHICAL READER.

WHAT WE LEARN IN GEOGRAPHY.

ge-og'-ra-phy. | de-scrip'-tion. | in'-ter-est-ing.

1. When we want to learn all about a thing, so as to be sure of making no mistake, we like to see and examine it for ourselves. We are not content to know only what others can tell us, for we feel that our eyes are our surest teachers.

2. That is the best way to learn many things about the EARTH; for we live upon it, and it is all around us, and before our eyes at all times. But the earth is so great, and most people travel so little, that they can see for themselves only a very small part of it, even if they use their eyes busily wherever they go.

3. There are a thousand things that every one wants to know about his country, and about other parts of the world, which he must learn by reading books. But these books tell us only what is on the outside, or *surface*, of the earth; for that is all that interests most people. A book which tells about the surface of the earth, and the people and countries upon it, is called a *Geography;* for geography means *a description of the earth*.

4. When we look around us, we see that the earth has two kinds of surface. One is firm and solid; and

we call it ground, or *land*. We walk or ride over it; we build our houses upon it; we see trees and grass growing out of it; we sow seeds in it, and soon it is covered with young, growing plants.

5. There is another part, which is not solid, but is always moving and flowing, and being stirred by the wind. This is *water*. People do not often build, upon

Land and Sea.

the water, houses to live in; but there is a sort of building made on purpose to move about on it, and to carry persons from place to place where they may wish to go. These moving houses are boats and ships. People found out how to build them, and to make the water useful in this way, almost as soon as they learned to build houses on the land.

6. We see more land than water, and it would not be at all strange if we should think there was more of it on the earth. But geography teaches us that there is much more water than land. Nearly *three fourths* of the earth's surface is water, and only about *one fourth* is land. This is one of the things which we could not see for ourselves if we should travel over all parts of the earth, and use our eyes carefully everywhere.

7. There are other things about the earth, which wise men found out only through many years of hard study. These, too, we must learn from books. One of these is the shape of the earth. People used, ages ago, to have queer ideas about this. They thought that the earth was flat, like a great plate; that it was held up in some wonderful way, and that the sun and the stars all traveled around it.

8. Now, the books teach us that the earth is a great ball; that it keeps all the time whirling round and round; and that, at the same time, it rolls on in a great journey about the sun, year after year, never stopping even for a single moment.

9. The geographies teach us, too, about interesting countries in far-off parts of the world; about strange people, who look very unlike us; and about strong and fierce animals and curious plants, which we have never seen, and which could not live in a country like ours.

10. Thus children who would become wise must learn how to study books, as well as how to use their own eyes at all times, and to think about what they see. But, if we learn about the earth only what the eyes of travelers can teach them, we shall know a great deal of geography, — more than most people know.

NORTH AMERICA.

I.—IN THE LEVEL COUNTRY.

jour′-ney [*jer′-ny*]. | car′-riage [*car′-rij*]. | veg′-e-ta-bles [*vej′-*].

1. Now for the geography which our eyes can teach us. To get this, we will begin by making a long journey in a carriage, using our eyes busily all the time as we go along.

2. At first, for many hours, we drive through a fine country, with pretty white farmhouses, orchards, and fields of grain; with broad green meadows where the haymakers are busy, and pastures where are flocks of sheep, and herds of cows and horses, feeding on the fresh sweet grass.

3. Little brooks ripple over the pebbles by the roadside, or wind, like silver threads, through the green grass of the pastures and meadows. Here and there are immense gardens, in which are raised great quantities of strawberries, melons, peaches, and other delicious fruits, and all sorts of vegetables for the table.

4. Now we drive through the pleasant, shady woods, where merry birds are singing, and many pretty flowers are blooming beneath the trees. We see squirrels hopping from branch to branch, or running as fast as their nimble feet can carry them, upon the fence by the

IN THE LEVEL COUNTRY. 5

roadside, and soon dodging out of sight into some heap of stones or brush.

5. By and by we come to a little village with its *church* and *schoolhouse*, and its *stores*, where the farmers come to sell their eggs and butter, and buy their sugar and tea, and the other things which they need.

In a Village.

6. There is not much to be seen, only the mill pond, which has been made by building a dam across one of the brooks we have passed, and the *mill* beside it, to which the farmers bring their grain. A little way off, are the *blacksmith's shop* and the *post office*, where three or four farmers are standing, talking over the news while waiting for their grain to be ground, or for their horses to be shod by the blacksmith.

7. Toward night we see the land before us rising higher and higher, so that if one above should loosen a stone, it would roll all the way down to us. Our horses begin to go slowly, for it is hard drawing the carriage up this road. Do you know what it is to which we have come? Of course you do. It is a *hill*, and we call it so because it is higher than the rest of the land. We first come to the *foot* of the hill; then we go up the *slope*, and finally we are at the *top*, and we shall soon begin to go down the other side.

II.—UPON THE HILLTOP.

| ho-ri′-zon. | At-lan′-tic. | o′-cean [-*shun*]. |
| pal-met′-to. | A-mer′-i-ca. | Pa-cif′-ic. |

1. LET us try what we can see from this hilltop. First look behind. There is the country through which we have been driving all the morning. There are many *farms* and *farmhouses;* many little *villages* scattered here and there, *roads* leading from one place to another in all directions, and *railroads* crossing the country in long, straight lines. There are also scattering *groves* that look very fresh and pleasant among the *gardens* and yellow *grainfields*, and *brooks* that shine in the sunlight like silver.

2. We can now see much more of the country than was in sight along the way as we were riding; because it is below us, and we can look down upon the whole of it at once. Compared with these hills, it seems quite flat and level; but there are many swells and hollows

UPON THE HILLTOP.

all over it. Do you know what to call a broad, low land like this? It is a *plain*.

3. You notice that the earth, at a distance from us as far as we can see, seems to be just against the sky. Do you suppose the sky comes down there and touches the earth? No, it only seems to do so. Look all around, and you will see that on every side it is the same. We

The Plain and Hills.

seem to be in the middle of a circle, with the sky touching the ground on all sides of us; just like a fly on a plate with a bowl turned over it.

4. You must remember that this *only seems* so. If you should go where the sky now appears to touch the earth, you would find it to be just as high, and just as far off, as ever. Some time, when you are older, you will understand why this is so; now you can only re-

member it. Try to remember, also, that the line where the earth and sky seem to meet, is called the *horizon*.

5. That part of the horizon where you see the sun rise, is called *east*. Where it sets, is *west*. The sun at noon is in the *south*, and high in the sky. Now, if you stand with your right hand toward the east and your left toward the west, you will face the *north*, and the *south* will be behind you. If you remember these points, you will always be able to know in what direction you are traveling, and can describe your journey so that other persons, who may wish to do so, can follow your route.

6. We came from the east. We are going toward the west. That plain which you see, stretches far away to the east, much beyond the place at which we started. We are now near the western border of it. Away on the eastern border, is an immense body of water. It is called the *Atlantic Ocean*, and this plain is called the *Atlantic Plain* because it borders upon the Atlantic Ocean. The part of the plain over which we have traveled is named *New Jersey*. It is only a very small part of the Atlantic Plain.

7. This great plain extends hundreds of miles to the north and the south, and is everywhere somewhat level; but it has not, in all parts, the same kinds of trees and animals, nor the same pretty farmhouses, villages, and smooth roads.

8. In some places, far away to the south, you will find, for miles and miles, nothing but tall, dark pine trees. There are no farms, no villages, but only the little cabins in which the people live who gather the turpentine from the pine trees.

IN THE LOW PLAIN.   9

9. In other places, still farther south, there are, for many miles, only great swamps. In these swamps are tall trees, with long moss trailing from the branches; and many kinds of flowers, growing in the water, like the white water lily.

A Rice Field.

10. In the parts which are not swampy, oranges and lemons grow; and the *palmetto*, which is very different from any of the trees in the north. It is a kind of palm tree, and can grow only in warm countries. In the lowlands, near the sea, you will find large fields of *rice*. When seen growing, it looks much like a field of wheat or tall grass.

11. Far to the south, there is no winter. Instead of skating and sleigh rides on Christmas and New Year's, people are working in their fields and gardens; and a few days later the ground is green with growing plants, and the roses and other flowers are in bloom. How would you like to live in such a place?

12. This great, rich, and beautiful plain is only one small portion of our country. Do you know what the name of our whole great country is? It is the UNITED STATES OF AMERICA. It reaches north and south as many as fifteen hundred miles, through the very best part of a great land, called *North America;* and it stretches east and west twenty-five hundred miles, from the borders of the Atlantic Ocean to another great ocean, called the *Pacific*.

III.—AMONG THE HILLS AND VALLEYS.

| Tren′-ton. | Del′-a-ware. | Phil-a-del′-phi-a. |
| Fair′-mount. | In-de-pend′-ence. | Schuyl′-kill [*Skool′-*]. |

1. WE have spent a long time on the hilltop, looking back toward the east, and studying the plain. Now we must go on with our journey. But the country through which we now pass is quite unlike that which we left behind us. It is not so pleasant to be going up and down, up and down, for hours together. But that is what we must do here; for there are many ridges to be crossed, and, almost as soon as we are over one, we find another to be climbed.

2. As we go down the long slope of this first ridge, do you notice the green belt of land at the bottom, before the slope begins to rise to the next ridge?

AMONG THE HILLS AND VALLEYS. 11

How pretty it is! And there, in the lowest part, is a lovely stream of water. These belts of lower land, between the higher grounds, are called *valleys*. If we were going along the valley, we could follow it for a long distance, by the side of its beautiful stream. Sometimes the hills on each side would be nearer, sometimes farther apart; and everywhere we should see farms and villages, just as we saw them in the

The City of Trenton.

plain farther east, for the valley is just like the plain, except that it is narrower.

3. We cross ridge after ridge, and valley after valley. Finally we descend a long, gentle slope; and there, spread out under our eyes, is a valley, wider and more lovely, and a stream greater, than any of those we have passed. This stream is named the *Delaware River;* for large streams are called rivers, and not brooks.

4. Here is a fine village on the river bank; and at this place we will take the railroad, and follow the

GEOG. READ. & PRIM.—2

valley toward the sea. We see, on the banks of the stream, several large and busy villages, and some still larger and busier places, called *cities*.

5. As the river goes on, it grows larger and larger; for brooks and smaller rivers, one after another, flow into it. Thus larger and larger vessels can sail on it, and more and more kinds of business can be done in the places on its banks. So we do not wonder at all when we come to cities that are bigger and more full of business than any which we have before seen.

6. Here is a city named *Trenton*. It is built just where the Delaware has become deep and wide enough for ships and steamboats to move about in its waters. We now change to another railroad. This carries us across the river, and on, southwestward, to a much greater city, built beside the Delaware, nearer the sea. This is *Philadelphia*, one of the largest cities in our country. It is in the State of *Pennsylvania*.

7. Here we see mile after mile of streets paved with blocks of stone to keep them firm and smooth. On each side of the streets, are walks which are thronged with people hurrying to and fro. In some of the streets, are lines of railroad. On the rails, are street cars filled with people who have too far to go, or are too much in haste, to walk.

8. Beside the streets, are long rows of tall houses, standing so close together that they touch one another, and look like only one great building. There is no room for flower gardens around the houses, such as we see in villages. The houses, too, are so much alike, that, if it were not for the number placed on each, a person might easily mistake some other house for his own.

AMONG THE HILLS AND VALLEYS. 13

9. On other streets there are rows of great stores, where thousands of people are busy all day, buying and selling all sorts of goods; and mills and factories, where other thousands are making nearly every kind of thing you could name. Railroads come to the city from almost every direction; and there are different stations, where the trains stop. At all these, are crowds of men

Broad Street Station, Philadelphia.

moving cars, or handling goods which are to be carried away on the railroads, or storing those which the cars have brought. At the wharves along the river, are other men working about the vessels which have come in, or are going out, laden with goods. Here, too, are hundreds of churches and schoolhouses, hotels and markets, and other buildings for the use of the people. What a wonderful place a great city is!

10. But, where many people live in one place, there are always some bad and troublesome persons, who must be kept from doing harm. So the city has policemen to look after them. Besides these, there are the mayor and aldermen, and many other officers, whose duty it is to attend to the public business. All these officers together make up what is called the *government* of the city. Philadelphia was founded and named by William Penn, in 1682, as the capital of Pennsylvania. Thus it is one of the oldest cities in the United States, as well as one of the largest.

11. There are many other things in Philadelphia which you would like to see and learn about, if there were time. There is the beautiful Fairmount Park, and there is an old building called "Independence Hall," in each of which something very interesting and important was done. Then there was a famous printer who lived here more than a hundred years ago. See what you can learn about these places, and about the famous old printer.

12. The *Schuylkill*, a small river which joins the Delaware, flows through Philadelphia. A number of fine bridges cross it, uniting the parts of the city which it separates. The Chestnut Street bridge is one of them.

IV.—AMONG THE MOUNTAINS AND MINES.

| gor'-ges. | Sus-que-han'-na. | Har'-ris-burg. |
| Penn-syl-va'-ni-a. | Ap-pa-la'-chi-an. | ma-chine' [-*sheen'*]. |

1. Now that we are ready to leave Philadelphia, we can take another train of cars, which will carry us westward as fast as we wish to go.

2. At first the road leads through a most beautiful country; and the pretty houses, and bright flowers, and smooth green fields, and lovely groves, seem like some pleasant park, rather than like the borders of a great city. By and by we find our way lying through rough hills. The road winds among them, finding break after break in the ridges, through which we cross from one valley to another.

3. At length we enter a broad valley, on each side of which is a great wall of very high land. Along the tops of these walls are *notches*, so that some parts are much lower than others; but even the lowest parts are much higher than any hill which we have yet seen. What can be the name of such land as this? You have heard of mountains, perhaps. Each of these *great solid walls of high land is a mountain range*. The higher parts are called *mountains*, or *peaks;* the lower, *passes*, that is, crossing places.

4. The mountains are much steeper, as well as higher, than the hills. They are also covered with great forests. Wherever we look, we see only trees, from the bottom to the top. What can be the reason the mountains are covered with forests, while on the plain and hills, and in the valleys, there is only here and there a little grove? There were once forests all over those regions, as well as upon the mountains; but they have been cut down to make room for the farms that now cover the land. We shall try, by and by, to learn why the forests have been left upon the mountains.

5. After a time we find a fine river, named the *Susquehanna*, flowing directly across the valley. It makes its way to the sea through breaks in the mountain

ranges, such as we saw in the hills from the cars. These are often just wide enough for the river to pass, and some are very grand. Such breaks are usually called *gorges*, but in these mountains they are also called *water gaps*.

6. On the Susquehanna, is the city of *Harrisburg*. If

On the Juniata Branch of the Susquehanna River.

we go about, to learn what the people are doing, we shall find, in all parts of it, great furnaces, where hundreds of men are at work, melting something that looks like black stone. Should you lift it, you would find it much heavier than stone. It is called *iron ore*, and is very abundant in the mountains and hills which we saw on our way here.

7. Iron is obtained from the ore by melting it in a furnace heated by *coke*. This *coke* is made from coal, which also abounds in the mountains of Pennsylvania. It is of great advantage to Harrisburg to be near the coal and iron mines, for on that account many people come here to live. The city contains large iron works, in which hundreds of men are constantly employed.

8. We now leave Harrisburg, and continue our way westward, across the valley. We soon reach the mountains, and can see how they are composed. They are not of soft earth, like the plain and the valley; nor of earth and rock mingled, like the hills: but they are made up of huge masses of rock piled together with only a very imperfect covering of soil upon them.

9. We called the mountain range a wall when we saw it at a distance. You see it is a solid stone wall. The rocks do not all look alike. Some are one great shapeless mass; and some are made up of layers, like very thick slates joined together. In some of these masses the layers are mostly level, like a floor; in others they are inclined, as if leaning one on another; and in still others they stand nearly erect, like the walls of a house.

10. What could have lifted them, and tossed them about in this way? You would not now understand if one should tell you. But you must try to remember how these rocks appear, and when you are older you will learn how they came to look as they now do. We wondered why the forests were left growing upon the mountains. It is because the mountains are so very rough and rocky that we could not well have farms and gardens upon them.

11. Now we have crossed the mountain range, and have entered another narrow valley, beyond which is another range, with its rounded peaks covered with forests. This, too, we cross; and, as we go on westward, we find other valleys and other ranges of the same kind, side by side, like great folds or wrinkles in the surface of the earth.

12. Now we reach the highest range of all. This we cannot cross through any gorge or valley; but we must climb the slope, and go over it. The road winds about, back and forth, up and up; and, when we are near the top, our train dashes into a tunnel cut through the solid rock, and comes out at the other end, ready to descend the long westward slope.

13. These ranges extend far to the south, and also to the north, almost to the borders of our country. If we should travel throughout their entire length we should find them everywhere very much alike, with their rounded summits and their covering of forests, and with long, narrow, and rich valleys between them. All of these ranges together are called a mountain *system*. This is the *Appalachian* mountain system. We shall find other mountains, very different from these.

14. Since we left Trenton, we have been in *Pennsylvania*. The mountains and hills of Pennsylvania contain immense beds of coal. They lie in separate, and sometimes very thick, sheets, with layers of rock above and between them. In some places they are deep in the earth; but in others they reach the surface, and their black edges can be seen between the beds of rock, in the mountain side or river banks. Places in which coal is taken out from under the ground are called *coal mines*.

15. When coal is found near the surface, it may very easily be taken out from between the layers of rock; but, when it lies deep, a hole, like a well, is dug down to it. This entrance is called a *shaft*. Now a machine for drawing up the coal is placed at the top of the shaft, and then the mine is ready for the workmen. They break the coal from the beds in large masses, which are drawn up the shaft, and afterwards crushed by machinery.

16. Beyond the last range of mountains, is the large city of *Pittsburg*. It is built where two small rivers unite, and form a greater one, named the *Ohio*. Pittsburg contains many great mills and forges, for working iron. The sound of the heavy machinery is never stilled, and night and day the busy hum of industry constantly fills the air.

17. Before we reach Pittsburg, we notice that the mountains gradually become lower and lower. Beyond it the country is made up of low ridges of hills, and wide, green valleys. It is very beautiful, with its pleasant groves and bright streams, among which are grain-fields and meadows, and pastures covered with horses, cattle, and sheep. In the country north of Pittsburg, are singular wells, from which *mineral oil* is pumped instead of water. *Kerosene* is made from this oil.

V.—IN THE ROLLING PLAINS.

| de-li'-cious. | un'-du-la-ting. | Cin-cin-na'-ti. |
| trans-por-ta'-tion. | to-bac'-co. | [Sin-sin-nah'-tī.] |

1. THE State lying next west of Pennsylvania is Ohio. It is a part of a great plain which lies on the west side of the Appalachian Mountains, but is very different from the Atlantic Plain. It is made up of low, rounded hills, not much higher than the rest of the land, with long, gentle slopes, and wide valleys between them. A surface of this kind, is called a *rolling*, or *undulating* plain.

2. This plain reaches westward for hundreds of miles, all through the middle part of the United States, stretching as far as the Rocky Mountains. For this reason, it has been named the *Great Central Plain*. But the different parts of it are very unlike. Most of the country is a rolling surface, like Ohio; but many parts are as level as the flattest portions of the Atlantic Plain.

3. These flat lands lie along the borders of rivers and great lakes, and were formed in some way by them, as the flat lands of the Atlantic Plain were made by the rivers and the ocean working together. When you are older, you can learn just how this was done; but now you could not understand it if you were told. Perhaps you can find out where some other flat plains lie, on the border of a distant ocean, where people find in the ground some very interesting things. Learn all you can about them.

4. As the country is unlike in different parts of the

Central Plain, so the kinds of work done, and the things which you will see growing, are very unlike. In some parts of it, are immense fields of wheat and corn, stretching, on every side, as far as the eye can reach. In other places, are pastures, where great herds of horses, sheep, cattle, and hogs, are feeding; and in

A Country View in Ohio.

still another part, the hillsides and valleys are planted with grapevines, from which the most delicious, juicy grapes are gathered. In some places they are produced in such quantities that they are carefully packed in small baskets and boxes, and shipped for use to different parts of the country where they are less abundant.

5. On the southern border of Ohio, in the midst of the rich and beautiful Ohio valley, is the great city of

Cincinnati. It is built beside the Ohio River, and is one of the busiest cities of the United States, being the center of a large trade for all the surrounding regions. Quantities of wool are marketed here, together with grain, meat, and other food supplies; and there is also a great amount and variety of manufacturing. Nearly all the year, boats are bringing coal

The Ohio River at Cincinnati.

from Pittsburg and bearing goods to and from the city.

6. All over the greater part of this plain, as well as on the Atlantic Plain, are large villages and cities, with multitudes of busy people. Some are working in mines, some are making all sorts of useful or beautiful articles, and some are buying and selling goods. All are very active at one thing or another.

7. But one of the greatest, the busiest, and most beautiful of the cities in Ohio, is *Cleveland*, on its northern border. It is situated on one of the finest harbors on the Great Lakes. Its leading branches of business are shipbuilding for the lake trade, and the manufacture of iron and steel from the rich ores brought from the Lake Superior iron mines.

VI.—ABOUT THE SPRINGS AND BROOKS.

Mis-sis-sip'-pi. | **I-tas'-ca.** | **is'-land** [*i'-land*].

1. The surface of the Great Central Plain is everywhere cut by green valleys, with clear, bright streams flowing through them, just as in the valleys among the mountains. Let us talk a little about these streams. We would like to learn whence they come, and whither they are going.

2. Do you remember ever seeing, on the sides of hills or mountains, places where the water comes from among the rocks, in little streams, cool and clear? We call them *springs*, you know. There are very many of them in all the hills and mountains that we have passed; and from every one, flows a little brook of clear, cool water. These brooks that flow through the little valleys, by and by flow together into one greater valley; and thus they form the rivers.

3. The Ohio River, on which Cincinnati is built, is formed by many smaller rivers, which are made by little brooks flowing from the springs in the Appalachian Mountains. But the hills and mountains are

earth and rock, not water. Where, then, can the water of the springs come from? Perhaps we shall learn that by and by. See if you can find it out.

4. Away in a forest of pine woods, almost on the northern border of our country, are a great number of springs. The hills from which these springs issue, are not high, steep, and rocky, like those near the Appalachian Mountains; but they are low and rounded, and made of sand and clay. Little streams flow from the springs in these hills, into a hollow, where they make a very small *pond*.

5. This pond is the place where the great *Mississippi River* begins its journey to the ocean. From it flows a little brook, so small, one could easily leap across it. You would hardly believe that this tiny stream would become, on its way to the ocean, a great river, large enough to carry heavy steamboats for thousands of miles.

6. Now, it cannot bear even a little boat, as it dances along over its gravelly bed, under the shadow of the pine woods. The banks on each side of the stream are covered with a soft carpet of bright green moss; and pretty wild flowers bend over the water. Many fallen trees lie across the brook; and low shrubs and bushes hang over it, so that, in some places, it is almost hidden by them.

7. After this brook has flowed a distance of six miles, it finds another small, basin-shaped hollow, into which it enters. Four other little streams flow into the same basin; and their waters spread out and fill it, forming a beautiful *lake*. This is *Itasca* Lake. It is usually called the *source*, or beginning, of the Mississippi; but

the real source is the tiny pond that is formed by the springs among the pines.

8. Some parts of the *shore* are low, almost even with the water; but in other places hills rise from the edge of the lake. The low shore is covered with bushes, grass, and flowers, and the hills, with tall pine trees. In the middle of the lake, is a small piece of land, also covered with tall trees. That is an *island*. You have perhaps seen islands in little streams in the woods and meadows.

9. If we were to come here in winter, we should find this place looking very different. The pretty lake, and all the streams flowing into it, would be covered with thick ice. The grass and low bushes would be buried out of sight, the flowers dead, and the pine trees wrapped in hoods and mantles of snow. Thus they sleep all through the long winter, until the return of spring awakens them to new life.

Itasca Lake.

VII.—ON THE UPPER MISSISSIPPI.

ca-noe' [-noo'].　　trib'-u-ta-ries.　　St. An'-tho-ny.
prec'-i-pice [pres'-].　　Min-ne-ap'-o-lis.　　[Saint An'-to-ni.]

1. IN order to learn something more about brooks and rivers, let us take a journey down the upper Mississippi, starting from Itasca Lake. But what shall we travel in? The river at first is not big enough to carry even the smallest kind of a steamboat or sailing vessel; so we must get a little boat called a *canoe*, which is moved by *paddles*. We shall easily find somebody to paddle us down the river.

2. Mile after mile we glide along, through the dark forest with its bright, sunny openings. We pass the *mouth* of many a smaller brook which pours its clear waters into the Mississippi, and so it grows larger and larger as we go on. These streams, which bring their waters to it, are called *tributaries* of the river.

3. We have now come to a place where great rocks lie in the middle of the stream, and the water foams and dashes through the narrow passages between them, so that we expect every moment to be driven against them, and have our boat broken to pieces. The current is so swift, that, in some places, the men cannot keep the boat off from the rocks with the paddles, but must wade in the stream to guide it through the narrow channels.

4. The bottom, or bed, of the river is very sloping; and that is the reason the water moves over it so rapidly, just as your sled goes more swiftly down a steep hill

than on a more gentle slope. The boatmen call this place the *Rapids*. Can you think why it is called so?

5. By and by we have passed the Rapids, and the river is broad and gentle; and, here and there, it spreads out into beautiful lakes, with green islands in them. Their shores of white sand glisten like snow in the sunshine; and trees of elm and maple, with bright green leaves and slender branches waving in the wind, make pretty groves upon their borders.

6. After we have gone on for many, many miles, we reach a place where the river is quite narrow, and the banks are somewhat steep. The boatmen tell us we must walk for a short distance; and, after we have left the canoe, they draw it up to the bank, and take it on their heads to carry it. I wonder what that is for. Perhaps, on our walk, we shall learn the reason of it.

7. We climb up the bank, and find a nice path through the forest. Do you hear that great roaring noise coming from the river? Let us go closer, and see if we can find what makes it. The banks here are very steep; and we must cling to the branches of the trees, or we may fall over.

8. Now look back, up the river. There is a place where the river's bed drops down suddenly, becoming much lower than before; and you see the waters come leaping and dashing down this long step, making a great foam and noise, just as you have seen them sometimes leap over a milldam.

9. This is called a *waterfall* or *cataract;* and the steep descent in the bed of the river is a *precipice*. You may have seen little falls in the brooks, among the meadows and woods; they are called *cascades*. Now

can you tell me why we have been obliged to walk? and why the boatmen took their boat out of the water, and carried it, instead of letting it carry them and us? The boat could not have come down the falls without being dashed to pieces, and we might all have been drowned.

A Cascade.

10. As we go on from this place, we find many rapids and falls hindering our way; and we pass among lovely islands in the bed of the stream, which has now deepened, and spread out into a large river. The country through which it flows is no longer covered with forests; but farms, villages, and cities take their place, just as on the rivers in the Atlantic Plain.

11. By and by, after many and many a day, we find

a busy, bustling city occupying both sides of the river, across which a number of bridges have been built. These are broad and strong, and make a way for railroads and street cars, as well as for people and carriages, to cross the stream, and great numbers of people pass continually.

12. This is the city of *Minneapolis;* and here are the Falls of St. Anthony, the last which the river makes in its course toward the sea. The people who first came here saw what a fine place this would be to build mills; for the water could be made to turn a vast number of mill wheels. And now the banks are crowded with mills, and the falls are hidden by timbers, so that one can hardly see any of the original view. Here our first river trip must end,—hundreds of miles from its beginning.

13. Only ten miles farther down the river, is another great city named *St. Paul,* to which we will go in a carriage. From St. Paul, the whole voyage to the sea can be made by steamboat.

VIII.—FROM ST. PAUL TO ST. LOUIS.

prai'-rie. | **dan'-ger-ous.** | **Mis-sou'-ri** [*soo'-*].

1. FROM the little lake which makes the cradle of the Mississippi, all the way to Minneapolis, groves of trees are everywhere in sight; and, once, nearly that whole country was covered with forests. Southward from this place, even before the white men came to cut down the trees, there were great treeless spaces, **cov-ered** with rich grass and bright flowers.

2. When the first white man saw these grassy plains along the Mississippi, he called them *prairies;* which, in his language, was the name for *meadows.* They were everywhere so smooth and green, and the low, round hills here and there, with their clusters of trees, looked so much like orchards, that it seemed almost as if people had lived here a great while ago, and planted these trees, and leveled these beautiful prairies.

A Prairie Farm.

3. One might have traveled many miles, east and west and south, and found them everywhere the same. Many beautiful birds hid in the grass, or went hopping about after the seeds and the insects on which they fed. There were also great herds of buffaloes, that fed upon the prairie grass; and curious little animals, called *prairie dogs*, made their burrows together, like the houses of a village.

4. Sometimes in the summer, when the grass was very dry, a little spark from a hunter's gun or pipe would set it on fire. Then the flame rushed over miles and miles of land, burning every blade of grass, and every tree and shrub; and even the animals could not always get out of the way of the fire, which went as fast as the wind. The burning prairie looks very grand; but when the flame is gone, and only the bare black earth is left, it is very dreary.

5. The prairie country, in winter, was sometimes one vast sheet of snow, with only here and there a house dotting it, and not a tree nor a fence to mark one place from another. It was very dangerous then for people to try to cross the prairies; for as the roads were covered with snow, and there was nothing to mark their place, travelers sometimes got lost, and were frozen to death.

6. Now all this is changed; and along the Mississippi and far westward, where once the wild prairies bloomed, there are busy cities, and pretty villages, and great farms with immense fields of wheat and corn, stretching as far as the eye can reach. Throughout the prairie country, the gently-sloping banks of the Mississippi are interrupted by steep walls, that rise on each side far above the water, as though a pathway had been cut for it, deep below the surface of the plain. These high steep slopes are called *bluffs*.

7. The bluffs do not rise close along both banks of the river. They are separated by a broad band of land, so low and flat as to be always overflowed when the water is a little higher than usual. This is called *bottom land*. Some parts of it are great marshes, covered with tall grass, or with thickets of cane that look

something like fields of corn, though the cane is much higher than the tallest corn. Other parts are covered with dense forests.

8. The river has now become very large; and, though there are no waterfalls or rapids, it still flows quite swiftly. Its course, too, is very winding. In some places, it glides in curves through the middle of the bottom lands; in others, its path is directly under the foot of the bluffs, which it is all the time washing and wearing away, carrying down to the sea the earth and rocks that fall from them.

9. Great trees, too, have the earth thus washed away from them, and are carried downward by the waters. Sometimes their roots become fastened to the bottom of the river, while their sharp tops, pointed down stream, reach nearly or quite to the surface. These are called *snags*, and are very dangerous; for steamers going up stream may easily run against them and be wrecked.

10. When we have gone about half the length of the Mississippi, and have passed many rivers flowing into it from both east and west, we reach the mouth of the *Missouri*, its largest tributary. This stream is much wider than that part of the Mississippi above it, and twice as long. Missouri means *great muddy;* and as the broad mass of muddy water comes pouring into the clear Mississippi, we do not at all wonder at the name.

IX.—ON THE LOWER MISSISSIPPI.

St. Lou'-is [Saint Loo'-is]. | plan-ta'-tions. | al'-li-ga-tors.
rep'-tiles. | New Or'-le-ans. | lev'-ee [lev'-y].

1. BELOW the mouth of the Missouri, is *St. Louis*, the largest city upon the banks of the Mississippi. It is also one of the largest and best located places in the United States. Its position on the Mississippi enables it to send boats from its wharves, not only to every city and village along this river, but also to those on the Missouri.

2. But this is not all. Not far below St. Louis, is the mouth of the *Ohio*, which is also a tributary of the Mississippi. By this stream, boats can be sent to Cincinnati and Pittsburg, and other places on its banks. Thus, by these three great rivers, and the smaller ones flowing into them, St. Louis can easily trade with every part of the rich plain through which they flow. Besides, like Cincinnati, railroads lead from this city in all directions. A long and handsome bridge, with railroad tracks as well as a carriage way, crosses the Mississippi here.

3. Below the mouth of the Ohio, the rich country through which the Mississippi flows begins to be covered with fields of cotton, instead of wheat and corn. In the spring, the young plant may be seen starting up from the seeds, in long lines across the fields. It grows rapidly, and puts forth branches like a little tree; and in summer it is covered with pretty pale-yellow flowers. Towards autumn, instead of flowers, there is a

34   *GEOGRAPHICAL READER.*

round fruit, looking somewhat like a walnut covered with its outside coat. When this fruit is ripe, it opens; and the long fibers of cotton, in which the seeds are wrapped, cover the plants like balls of snow.

4. Now hundreds of negro men and women may be seen in the fields, picking the cotton carefully from the pod with their fingers. This is very slow work; and,

Cotton Picking.

as the cotton balls are not all ripe at the same time, it lasts a long while. After the cotton is picked, it is dried, and the seeds are all taken out. This is done by a machine called a cotton gin, which works very rapidly. Finally, the snowy mass is packed in great bundles, or *bales*, and is ready to be sent to the cotton mills, to be made into cloth.

5. The country on each side of the lower Mississippi, for hundreds of miles from its mouth, is very low and flat. It is one great plain of black earth and sand, in which not even a single stone can be seen. The parts near the river are a little higher than the rest; and they are covered with great plantations of sugar cane, looking like fields of corn. Farther from the river, are immense marshes covered with canebrakes and tall trees.

6. Every year, in the spring and early summer, the streams overflow their banks; and these marshes become lakes, in which only the tops of the trees can be seen. Often villages would be washed away, plantations covered, and everything destroyed, were it not for walls, called *levees*, which are built on the banks of the river to make them higher, and prevent overflowing. Sometimes these levees are broken, and the lands behind them are covered with water, and many people are drowned.

7. This is a warm country, like the southern part of the Atlantic Plain. The marshes and streams are thronged with alligators, snakes, turtles, and other *reptiles*; and the air swarms with troublesome *insects*.

8. Towards the mouth of the Mississippi, with the sugar plantations all about it, is the great city of *New Orleans*. To this place the planters bring their sugar and molasses, to be put upon steamboats or sailing vessels, and sent to parts of the country where sugar cane is not raised. Boats and cars come here, too, loaded with cotton from the plantations farther up the river. This, also, is sent to other parts of our own country, or across the ocean to distant countries, where it is used

to supply the mills. Thus you see that this, too, is a very active city. It is also a curious old town. You will like to learn more about it when older.

9. We have now traveled all the way from the source of the Mississippi to its mouth, about one hundred miles below New Orleans. This river is so very

On the Levee at New Orleans.

long, that should we start from its source in the spring, just after the snow is gone, and travel twenty miles every day, it would be nearly fall before we should arrive at its mouth. There are but very few rivers in the whole world longer than the Mississippi. The part of the sea into which it flows, lies upon the south side of the United States, and is called the *Gulf of Mexico.*

10. Ships from other countries cross the Atlantic Ocean and the Gulf of Mexico, and go up the Mississippi to New Orleans. There they unload their cargoes. Some of the goods are used in the city; and some are put on steamboats, and sent up the river to other places. These steamboats return to New Orleans, loaded with lumber, wheat, corn, tobacco, cotton, and other things, which are to be shipped to countries across the ocean.

11. Thus, you see, the rivers help to make a pathway, not only between different parts of our country, but also to other countries beyond the ocean. This it is which makes large rivers so important.

X.—AT THE MOUTH OF THE HUDSON.

Hud'-son. | In'-di-an. | an'-chor [an'-ker].

1. There is, in the northern part of the United States, another river, which, though it is only about half as long as the part of the Mississippi above the Falls of St. Anthony, yet is nearly as important as the Mississippi itself. It is the *Hudson*. It flows from north to south through the eastern part of the State of New York. At its mouth is NEW YORK, the largest city in America.

2. Boats come down the Hudson to New York, bringing loads of wheat and corn from the great grainfields on the prairies, loads of lumber from the forests near the sources of the Mississippi, and many other products coming from the west by the great lakes on the north-

ern border of the United States. By the same route, the silks, coffee, and tea, and other merchandise brought to New York in ships, from countries across the ocean, are forwarded to their places of destination in the north and west. The Hudson is therefore much more important than most other rivers of its size; and is more useful than many that are much larger.

New York Harbor.

3. NEW YORK, though it is one of the largest cities in the world, is not nearly so old as most cities in other countries. The first houses were built there not quite three hundred years ago, by some Dutch people who came from a country on the other side of the Atlantic Ocean.

4. Then the great plain east of the Appalachian Mountains, which is now covered with farms, pretty

villages, and fine cities, was everywhere one unbroken forest. In the shade of these forests, lived many beautiful birds and some large and strong ones, like the eagle. There were many fierce wild animals, — bears, wolves, and panthers; and there were many harmless ones, like the deer.

5. The Indians, also, lived in these forests. Their huts were the only houses the Dutch strangers found; and their bark canoes, the only boats on the Hudson. The Indians did not like to have the white people come to live in their country; because they cut down the forests, built houses, and plowed and planted the fields, and thus frightened away the wild animals. They, therefore, burned the houses of the Dutch, and killed many people. In this way they tried to drive them away, or to prevent their making themselves comfortable, and increasing in numbers.

6. But they did not succeed. More Dutch people came every year; and, by and by, English people came also. The little village grew into a great town; the town increased in size as the years passed, and at length became a city. Fine, large buildings were put up; new streets, broad and straight, were opened; and pretty parks were laid out. And thus, after many years, New York, which began with a dozen or two little log houses, has become the great city it now is.

7. In the broad mouth of the river, beside the city, are hundreds and hundreds of ships from all parts of the world. Some are moved by the wind blowing against sails; others are great steamers, much larger and stronger than those on the Mississippi. Some are used to carry goods and passengers from one place to

another; others are war ships, carrying soldiers, and great, heavy, terrible cannons.

8. Here, also, are large steamboats which run only upon the Hudson. Some of these Hudson steamers are very elegant, and move over the water with great speed. We shall presently get into one of them, and make a journey up the river.

9. Many vessels lie quietly on the water, held in place by a strong, heavy *anchor*, which is fastened to the ship by a great rope, called a *cable*. When the master of the ship wishes to remain in the same place for some time, he has the anchor thrown into the water; and it sinks to the bottom, fastens itself to the earth by its strong hooks, and holds the ship securely. This place in which the ships are lying at anchor, is called the *harbor*.

10. There are islands, near the mouth of the river, that keep the great waves of the sea from rolling into the harbor; and the high lands, on each side of it, prevent the winds from blowing very hard upon the ships. Thus, they are in no danger of being dashed about and broken to pieces, as they might be in the ocean. New York Harbor is one of the largest and safest in the world.

XI.—UP THE HUDSON.

per-pen-dic'-u-lar. | aq'-ue-duct [ak'-we-]. | Al'-ba-ny.
Pal-i-sades'. | car'-goes. | Ad-i-ron'-dacks.

1. At nine o'clock on a beautiful spring morning, we make our way to the place where the Hudson River steamers are to be found, and go on board one of them. The sunlight falls on the sails that skim the harbor, and makes them white as snow; and the tall domes and spires of the city glitter like silver.

2. We pass miles of wharves lined with vessels which are receiving or discharging their cargoes, and of streets, some bordered with low, dirty-looking shops, some with tall, handsome buildings. Here and there, are large factories with dull brick walls and smoking chimneys. Now we begin to know what a great city New York is. At length the shops and wharves and straight, paved streets, are all passed, and we are steaming along through the country.

3. On the east bank of the river, are elegant country houses, surrounded by trees, with pretty walks winding down the green slope to the water's edge. There are dark evergreens with their tall, stiff figures, and graceful elms and maples, with their delicate green leaves dancing in the morning wind. There are other trees, covered with snow-white flowers, with scarcely a leaf to be seen. The ground is smooth, and the grass thick and green, showing that somebody has taken care of these lands, and spent much time and money to make them beautiful.

4. The west side looks very different. There rises, near the river's edge, a great perpendicular wall of naked rock, reaching very much higher than the tallest tree. It begins opposite the upper part of New York, and extends several miles up the river.

5. This wall is called the *Palisades*. That sloping bank seen at its foot, is made of pieces of rock that occasionally fall from above. Here and there, at the foot of the slope, is a little cottage or other small building; but there are none of those fine houses and parks that make the other bank so beautiful.

6. Just above the Palisades, the river spreads out into a broad sheet, like a lake. This is called *Tappan Bay*. The

Palisades of the Hudson.

banks are high, and covered with handsome houses and parks, like those already seen; and here and there, are pretty little villages almost hidden by trees. Beyond the villages, are fine farms, with orchards covered with their fragrant pink and white blossoms. Plowmen and sowers are working in the fields; and flocks of

UP THE HUDSON.

sheep and lambs, and herds of cows, are feeding upon the hillsides.

7. At the upper end of Tappan Bay, the *Croton*, a little river of bright, pure water, flows into the Hudson. It comes from small lakes far away among the hills east of the Hudson. From the Croton, water is carried, in a great tube called an *aqueduct*, all the way to the city of New York, and is sent through pipes into the houses and other buildings; for, in a great city where so many people live, they cannot have springs and wells of pure water, as in the country.

8. After a time, the Hudson becomes very narrow, and changes its course, so that we can see it only for a short distance ahead. On both sides, great mountains come down to the water's edge, with their steep, rocky slopes covered with forests of evergreens. The river seems to be coming to an end at the foot of these mountains.

Highlands of the Hudson.

9. As we go on, a narrow passage opens between them, — so narrow that one could almost toss a stone from the boat to either bank. Through this passage, the river rushes very swiftly, and the people here call this place the *Horse Race*. For a long distance, the river keeps this narrow path, with the mountains on each side of it. All this mountain region together, is called the *Highlands of the Hudson*.

GEOG. READ. & PRIM.—4

10. In the Highlands, on a part of the mountain side which is less steep, is West Point, of which you will hear and read many interesting things as you become older. Opposite West Point, is the narrowest part of the Hudson. Many years ago our country was at war with England, and the English had possession of New York. Our people then built strong forts here, with heavy guns pointing over the river, to fire on the English ships if they should attempt to go up the stream to destroy the cities and villages along its banks.

11. Beyond the Highlands, for many miles, the high, sloping banks of the river are again covered with fine farms and elegant buildings, with villages and cities here and there. Soon the distant *Catskill* Mountains appear in the west, like a bank of purple clouds. They do not approach very near to the river, but in some places can be seen quite plainly.

12. Above the Catskills, the river contains many islands. Some are rocky and covered with trees, and look like little hills in the middle of the stream. Others are very flat, and covered with low plants.

13. After some hours, we reach *Albany*, the largest city on the Hudson above New York. It is built on a number of hills extending back from the river, rising one beyond another; so that, in passing, a great part of the city can be seen. On the top of one of these hills, surrounded by fine old elms, is a large building in which, every winter, chosen men, from all parts of the State meet to make the laws that govern its people. Because they meet here, Albany is called the *capital* of New York. The building in which they meet is named the *Capitol*.

14. Six miles above Albany, there is a smaller city, named *Troy*. Here, as in Harrisburg and Pittsburg, are great furnaces and iron works. We have now been from early morning until late afternoon upon the river, and have gone from New York to Troy, one hundred and fifty miles.

15. We can go no farther than Troy on the steamer, for here the stream becomes too small, and, like the upper Mississippi, its course is filled with rapids and waterfalls. The finest of these is *Glens Falls*. There, and at the other rapids and falls, are mills of different kinds, the wheels of which are moved by the water of the river. Thus the upper Hudson, as well as the lower and larger part, is very useful. Its source is far away in the northern part of the State, among high, rugged mountains called the *Adirondacks*.

16. Nearly every part of the Hudson thus lies among mountains. Above the Palisades, mountains — sometimes near at hand, sometimes far off — are in sight of the river through the whole distance to its source. Along the entire length of the Mississippi, nearly ten times that of the Hudson, there is not a single mountain range; the bluffs are the only high land to be seen. The Mississippi is the river of the Great Plain, but the Hudson is a mountain river.

17. The Hudson has only one large tributary, the *Mohawk*. It flows from the west, and enters the Hudson near Troy. The Mohawk valley is full of fine farms, and covered with pretty villages; and along the river are busy cities. The Dutch, who founded New York, made settlements about the mouth of the Mohawk; and some of their fine old mansions are still to be seen.

XII.—THE ERIE CANAL AND THE GREAT LAKES.

Mack'-i-nac [*-naw*]. | **Mich'-i-gan** [*Mish'-*]. | **Chi-ca'-go** [*-kaw'-*].

1. From Albany, a canal has been made through the Mohawk valley, connecting the Hudson with Lake Erie. It is a broad, deep channel filled with water, on which boats run between the river and the lake. Lake Erie is one of the five Great Lakes which extend along the northern border of the United States. By the Hudson, the Erie Canal, and the Great Lakes, we have a water route all the way from New York to the great grainfields on the prairies.

2. Canal boats, loaded at New York, are towed by steamboats up the river, and are drawn on the canal by horses walking on a *towpath* beside it. At length they reach *Buffalo*, a large city at the east end of Lake Erie. The goods are now taken from them, and put upon larger boats which sail upon the lakes; and the canal boats are loaded with grain, lumber, and other freight, and sent back to New York.

3. Lake Erie is very different from the little lakes found among the hills on the upper Mississippi. It is much longer than the whole distance from New York to Troy; and it is so wide, that, if we were in the middle of it, we could scarcely see land on either side.

4. Sometimes, when the wind blows hard, the water is lifted up in great ridges, with deep hollows between them, like little hills and valleys in the lake. These movements of water are called *waves*, and they heave

THE ERIE CANAL AND THE GREAT LAKES. 47

the large vessels about as easily as you could toss an eggshell in your hand. Sometimes vessels, driven ashore, are dashed to pieces by them; and all the people on board are drowned, and all the goods lost.

The Mohawk Valley and the Erie Canal.

The southern side of Lake Erie belongs to the United States; and along its shores, are cities and villages, where the steamers stop to receive or land passengers and goods.

5. At the west end of Lake Erie, a short river enters it from the north. It comes from *Lake Huron*, and

widens in the middle, forming *Lake St. Clair.* Lake Huron is nearly three times as large as Lake Erie. In it are many large, beautiful islands covered with trees; and, in almost its whole extent, it is bordered with forests like those about the source of the Mississippi. There are no large cities, and but few villages, on its shores. After we have gone the entire length of Lake Huron, we enter a narrower body of water, named the *Strait of Mackinac.* Through this we enter *Lake Michigan.*

6. Lake Michigan is the smaller one of two great lakes which we can enter from the head of Lake Huron. It extends far toward the south, and much of its shore, in the northern part, is covered with forests. All around the southern part, are villages and cities, which are every day sending out vessels loaded with lumber from the forests, or with produce from the farms. At its head, is *Chicago*, one of the greatest cities in America.

7. The grain, flour, beef, and pork produced in the regions around, and even far west of, the Mississippi are brought here in immense quantities, and forwarded to New York. From this place, they can easily be sent, in ocean ships, to all parts of the world. Since there are railroads in every direction, Chicago trades with other cities, as well as with New York, to which it has this easy waterway by the lakes, the canal, and the Hudson.

8. *Lake Superior* is the other great lake which is connected, by a short and narrow stream, with Lake Huron. On its shores, also, are pine forests. In some places on the south shore, there rise from the water's edge high walls of rocks of strange forms and different colors. These are called the *Pictured Rocks.*

9. Parts of the shore are very high and steep; and in one place a river, in entering the lake, falls over the steep precipice, making a beautiful waterfall. When there are storms, the waves dash against these rocks with great fury; and, if there should be vessels in that part of the lake, they would be almost sure to be wrecked, for there is no sheltered harbor in which they could find safety.

10. This is one of the largest lakes of fresh water known in the whole world. It spreads out on all sides, like a great sea. A steamer is two or three days in going from one end of it to the other, and, in the middle parts, is out of sight of land, as though in the middle of the ocean. There are not so many vessels seen on this lake as on the other

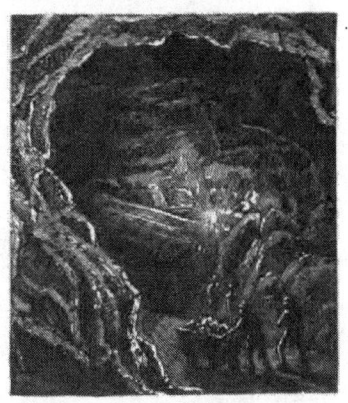

Copper Mining.

three; and there are but few cities along its border.

11. On the south shore, there are large mines of copper, in which hundreds of men are at work all the time. Sometimes great lumps of pure copper are found, with no rock, or other substance, mingled with it, but all ready for use. This is called *native copper*. Rich iron ore, also, is found on the south shore; and all summer one may meet, on the lakes, vessels loaded with it. Ore is sent from these mines to cities on the shores of the other lakes, and even to more distant

places, where there are furnaces for separating the metal.

12. Toward the foot of the lake, near Lake Huron, many people are engaged in catching white fish, which are abundant here. In the forests along the shores, are many wild animals which used to be hunted for their furs. Among these is the *beaver*. Do you know how he builds his home upon the streams?

Beavers at Work.

13. At the western end of Lake Superior, the *St. Louis River* enters it. This stream has its source very near that of the Mississippi, in the same forest-covered hills; and, like that river, its waters find their way, through a long, long course, to the Atlantic Ocean.

XIII.—LAKE ONTARIO AND THE ST. LAWRENCE.

La-chine' [-*sheen'*]. | **Mon-tre-al'** [-*awl'*]. | **Mont-mo-ren'-ci** [-*se*].

1. FROM the east end of Lake Erie, a passage, called *Niagara River*, leads northward to another great basin,

The American Fall, from the Canadian Bank.

Lake Ontario. About half way between these lakes, are the great Niagara Falls.

2. This broad mass of water is of a pale green color; the boiling, rolling stream below is snowy white; while the clouds of mist show, in the sunshine, all the colors of the rainbow. In the middle of the fall, is an island, crowned with evergreen trees; and its black rocks divide the beautiful green waters into two broad sheets.

3. The broad green wall of waters, the white foamy mass below, the black rocks, and the dark green foliage, with the roaring, thundering noise of the rushing waters, present a grand and wonderful scene,

4. *Lake Ontario* is the last and the smallest of the five Great Lakes, and the only one that has both shores bordered everywhere with farms, villages, and cities. The southern shore belongs to the United States, and the northern to the *Dominion of Canada*. From the eastern end of this lake, the water flows northeastward to the Atlantic, in a great stream called the *St. Lawrence*. At the point where it leaves the lake, is a city on the Canada shore named *Kingston*. From this place, steamers are every day going around the lake, and down the river, stopping at all the important places.

5. The part of the river near the lake is filled with a great number of islands, — some quite large, and others very small. They were once all covered with tall forest trees, and are reflected in the quiet waters as in a mirror, making a very beautiful picture. This part is called the *Lake of the Thousand Islands*.

6. Below the Thousand Islands, the river is broad and gentle for a long distance, with fine forests on both sides of it, and only here and there a village on the banks. Farther on, the banks become higher and steeper, and the river more swift; and we enter the great rapids. In the middle of the stream, are many islands; and the river foams and dashes through the narrow channels, carrying our boat with it. It needs several strong men to guide it so that it shall not strike the rocks in its passage. These are the *Lachine* Rapids.

7. We could not go up the rapids as we have come down; for the water would force the boat back as fast as the steam could drive it forward. For this reason, a canal has been cut around the rapids, for vessels which are going up stream.

LAKE ONTARIO AND THE ST. LAWRENCE. 53

8. A little below the Thousand Islands, the river leaves the border of the United States, and goes across the *Dominion of Canada* to the ocean. There are not upon its banks such numbers of villages and cities as along the Mississippi and the Hudson; for this part of

The Citadel of Quebec.

the Dominion is rather cold, and does not contain many people. The country is, in many parts, still covered with forests where only hunters, Indians, and wild animals live.

9. The largest city on the St. Lawrence is *Montreal*, a little way below Lachine Rapids. It is situated at the foot of a mountain, on an island. Opposite the upper end of the island, a large stream, called the *Ottawa*, flows into the St. Lawrence from the north.

10. *Quebec*, another city on the St. Lawrence, is built

at the mouth of the *St. Charles*, about one day's journey for a steamboat, below Montreal. It stands on the point of land made by the meeting of the two rivers. Next the river, the ground is nearly as low as the stream; but farther back, it rises in a steep bluff.

11. Quebec is built partly on the low, and partly on the high land. The Upper Town — that is, the part on the hill — contains a strong fort called the *citadel*, and is surrounded by a great wall with five gates. In the citadel, are soldiers whose duty it is to defend the town if an enemy should attack it.

12. Looking about you from the citadel, you see, in front, the river spread out like a broad lake, its surface dotted with vessels, with now and then a steamer hurrying to and fro, or a raft of lumber floating slowly down the stream.

13. Below you is the Lower Town, having on one side the broad St. Lawrence, and on the other the small, beautiful St. Charles. Behind, away in the distance, are green hills and forest-covered mountains, and, stretching away to the east as far as you can see, the great river, becoming always broader and broader, until it seems to be itself another lake going to the sea; for it soon becomes half as wide as Lake Erie.[1]

14. The French people began to build this town, long before the Dutch commenced New York; and though the English took it from them in time of war, there are still many French people living here, and French is more spoken than English.

15. The summers in Quebec are quite warm; but the

---

[1] The St. Lawrence just below Quebec is twelve miles in width; but, long before it reaches the Gulf, it has a width of near thirty miles.

winters are long, and very, very cold. The snow is deep; and the small lakes and rivers, and even the great St. Lawrence, from Montreal all the way to the sea, are frozen over for several months. Then people drive about upon them in sleighs, instead of sailing in boats as in summer.

16. When the spring comes, and the ice in the St. Lawrence begins to break up, the sight is very grand. Great blocks of ice are carried down stream by the water; for the upper part, nearest the lake, feels the warm weather first; and they are sometimes heaped one upon another, until immense masses are formed. The strongest bridges are often broken away by the drifting ice.

17. A few miles below Quebec, a small river, called the *Montmorenci*, flows into the St. Lawrence. The banks of the great river are here very high; and the water of the Montmorenci makes a long leap to get from its own bed down to the St. Lawrence. As you sail along, you do not see the small river, which is far above, and hidden by the bank,— you see only the water pouring over a great precipice, higher than that of Niagara, as if coming from the clouds. These are the *Falls of Montmorenci*.

18. In winter the falls are very grand, and many people go from Quebec to see them. The ground is buried in snow; and the branches of the evergreen pines and firs are bending under its weight. The leafless trees, even to every little twig, are covered with ice; and when the sun rises in the morning, and shines upon them, they glisten like a forest of diamonds.

19. The precipice, too, is covered with ice; and the mist which rises from the bottom, as at Niagara, freezes,

and forms steep hillocks of ice. People drive to Montmorenci from Quebec, to go skating, or to climb the ice hills and slide down their steep slopes.

20. From this place to the ocean, the river flows on, broad and majestic, with forests covering the whole country around, and on both sides mountains rising in the distance. In these forests, are many wild animals, some of them covered with the finest fur. Many trappers hunt them for their furs, which are made into warm wraps, for use in the long, cold winters.

XIV. — LAKE CHAMPLAIN AND THE ADIRONDACKS.

| Cham-plain'. | Rich'-e-lieu. | New Eng'-land. |
| [Sham-]. | [Re-she-loo']. | [Ing'-]. |

1. In following the St. Lawrence to the sea, we were obliged to leave our own country and go into Canada. There is a pleasant part of our country south of the St. Lawrence, which we could not see on this journey.

2. Between Montreal and Quebec, there is a river, named *Richelieu*, flowing northward into the St. Lawrence, from *Lake Champlain*, which lies between New York and New England. At the upper end of this lake, is a smaller, but more beautiful one, the water of which flows into Lake Champlain. This is *Lake George*.

3. These lakes have clear blue water, with many little islands rising from the surface, covered with evergreen trees. On their shores, are forest-covered mountains and hills, which, with the islands, are all pictured in the quiet waters below; and away in the distance, on both sides, are other and higher mountains, that make a

framework of green for the clear, bright lakes. Many people go every summer from New York and other cities, and live in little villages on the shores of these lakes, to enjoy the views, and sail on the clear waters.

4. The high mountains west of Lake Champlain are the *Adirondacks*. They belong to the Appalachian system, but are much higher and rougher than the mountains of Pennsylvania. If you were on the top

Lake George.

of one, and looking over the country, you would see mountain beyond mountain, stretching away on every side, like the waves of a great rolling sea.

5. The whole country is covered with grand old forests, just as it was before the white people came. Here and there, on the steep sides of the mountains, you see large spaces of bare rock. These were once, like the rest, covered with trees. At some time, after a long rain, the earth upon these rocks became loosened from its place, and went sliding down the mountains,

carrying all the great trees with it to the foot, leaving the mountain side bare and drear, as you now see it.

6. In the hollows among the mountains, are hundreds of small lakes, whose black waters reflect the mountains, the forests, and the sky as perfectly as the finest mirror. If you were upon one of these lakes in the nighttime, you could see the sky and the moon and stars below you just as distinctly as above.

7. There are very few villages or farms in this moun-

The Adirondacks.

tain country. These regions still belong in great part to the wild beasts; and bears, wolves, and deer, with hundreds of smaller animals, roam through them at will.

8. There are rich ores of iron in all parts of the Adirondacks; but some of the richest beds are away in the midst of the mountains, where the country is so rough that they cannot easily be reached for working. In the region around the mountains, are villages and cities, where the people are melting ore, or making articles from iron, as in Pennsylvania.

XV.—NEW ENGLAND.

Bos'-ton. | Brook'-lyn. | Ches'-a-peake [-*peek*].
Con nect'-i-cut [-*net'-*]. | Bal'-ti-more [*Bawl'-*]. | Po-to'-mac.

1. THE part of our country east of the valley in which Lake Champlain and the Hudson River lie, is called *New England*. There is first a range of forest-covered mountains, extending away to the south much farther than the lake itself. This is the beautiful *Green Mountain* range. East of this, is a long valley extending southward by its side.

2. This is not a level valley; but it is covered with low, green hills. In every part of it we see fine farms, and pretty, busy villages and cities. In the middle of the valley, winding along its whole length, is the *Connecticut River*. Its pleasant banks are dotted with farmhouses, surrounded by green meadows, orchards, and fields of grain.

3. Beyond the valley, is another ridge of land, on the northern part of which is a knot of mountains somewhat like the Adirondacks, but much higher than they. These are the *White Mountains*. Mount Washington is the highest of them. The high peaks near it are named for other presidents; and it is common to call this whole group the *Presidential Range*.

4. All over New England, are green hills and fruitful valleys, or forest-covered mountains with beautiful glassy lakes, as in the Adirondacks. From these, flow silvery streams, which go dancing along, adown the hills and mountains, to the sea. On their banks, are villages, crowded with mills whose wheels are turned

by the swift waters; and great cities, filled with busy people who are sawing, hammering, spinning, weaving, grinding, and making all sorts of things, — working away as though they had twice as many things to do as they could possibly find time for.

5. On the seashore, too, are large cities. Here they

White Mountains.

are building great ships to sail on the ocean, or loading them with lumber from the forests, ice from the mountain lakes (for it is very cold here in winter), and boots and shoes, and cloth, and all sorts of goods. Thus they send these things to market, and bring back cotton for their mills, sugar and tea and coffee for their tables, and many other things which they need. Other vessels go toward the mouth of the St. Lawrence, to the fishing grounds, or take brave men away to the distant parts of the ocean to catch whales.

6. The rivers are full of rapids and falls, and very few are large enough for vessels to sail upon; but there are railroads all over the country, to carry the goods from place to place. Everywhere are fine schools, in which

The City of Boston.

children and young people can learn whatever they need to make them wise and useful.

7. The largest of the cities in New England is *Boston*. This city was founded in 1630, only ten years after the "Pilgrim Fathers" came to Plymouth in the "Mayflower." You will, as you become older, hear of many beautiful and interesting things which are in Boston, and of many famous men who have lived there.

8. At this city we will take one of the New England steamers, and sail southward along our whole Atlantic coast. On the way we shall pass *Brooklyn,* one of the boroughs of New York. It is on *Long Island,* and is separated from the chief borough, Manhattan, by the *East River.* Boats go every few minutes from Manhattan to Brooklyn, carrying thousands of people every day. Other thousands daily cross on the great suspension bridge between the boroughs. Very many people who live in Brooklyn have their places of business in Manhattan.

9. Farther south, are *Philadelphia* and *Baltimore,* neither of which is upon the seashore, but ships can easily reach both. They are near parts of the ocean called *bays;* which extend, like arms, away from its great body, far into the land. Philadelphia is near *Delaware Bay,* into which the Delaware River flows. Baltimore is near *Chesapeake Bay,* on a river which flows into it.

10. South of Baltimore the *Potomac* flows into this bay. Upon the Potomac is WASHINGTON, a city of great interest to us. There the President lives, and every year men chosen from the different States meet there to make laws for the whole country; for Washington is the capital of the United States.

11. Still farther south, upon the seashore, are several fine cities, though no very large ones. Here we pass the turpentine forests, the palmetto groves, the cotton fields, the swampy rice lands, and the immense marshes of the southern part of the Atlantic Plain, with their trailing moss and their water plants, their alligators and their swamp birds.

12. Here, also, are forests of the *live oak*, the wood

of which is very durable, and is excellent for building ships. Now we sail along the coast of *Florida*, the most southern State of our country. Finally we turn westward, pass into the Gulf of Mexico, and at length arrive at New Orleans.

13. We have now seen the eastern half of the United States, the part in which are very many of the great cities, and in which a large part of the people live. Everywhere we have found rich farms, fine forests, or fruitful prairies; and in every part, are rivers and lakes, some small, others so very large that we can sail upon them hundreds and even thousands of miles.

14. This half of the United States, with its rich lands, its great lakes, and long rivers, extends beyond the Mississippi, almost half way to the foot of the Rocky Mountains. You will find the western half very different; but I hope it will interest you to learn something about it.

XVI.—IN THE ROCKY MOUNTAIN COUNTRY.

buf'-fa-loes. | **pas'-ture.** | **Den'-ver.**

1. THE prairie land, beginning along the Mississippi, extends westward to the Rocky Mountains, the limit of the Great Central Plain. The far western prairies, however, are not all rich and beautiful like those along the Mississippi, but are high, and, in many parts, dry and naturally barren. On these prairies herds of *buffaloes* used to feed, and the wild Indians used to roam. They lived in little huts, and spent their time in hunting and fighting. They hunted the buffaloes for the

flesh, which they used for food; and for the **skins**, which they sold to white people.

2. When the buffaloes had eaten all the grass from one portion of the prairies, they went to another, where they found it fresh and green. The Indians, knowing where the best pastures were, and when the herds would go to each, followed them, — some to one place, and some to another. They went in companies, and staid until the buffaloes had finished feeding in that place.

An Indian Lodge.

3. When they went to the hunt, they rode on their fleetest horses; for the buffaloes run very swiftly. Many hunters usually went out together, and, when they had found a herd, surrounded the place, drove them together,

and killed them in great numbers. Sometimes, too, they drove them swiftly to the edge of a precipice, over which they fell, and hundreds at a time were killed. The Indians were very fond of this way of hunting.

4. The *Rocky Mountains* are quite different from any mountains in the eastern half of the United States. If you could look down upon them from above, you would see two great ranges, side by side, with a wide valley between them. They are so lofty that their lowest passes are higher than the highest peaks of the Appalachians. Many short ranges, crossing between them, cut up the great inner valley into broad basins, some of them dark with forests, and others bright with rich prairie grass. All the lower and middle slopes of these mountains are thickly covered with forests.

Rocky Mountains.

5. Higher up, the trees become smaller and smaller, until only bare gray rocks appear, with here and there patches of grass or of bright mountain flowers. Above these, are the high, wild peaks, covered with snow even in summer, and glistening above the dark forests and rocks like crowns of silver. These peaks have all sorts of rugged, broken forms; and the whole mountain sys-

tem looks as though the earth's crust had been all torn and broken in pieces, instead of gently folded, as it appeared in the Appalachians.

6. You would hardly suppose people could wish to live among the Rocky Mountains; but large numbers of men are there, and more are going every year. Great herds of cattle are pastured in the valleys between the ranges; and in the mountains, are rich mines of silver and gold, with towns growing up around them. *Denver*, at the eastern side of the mountains, is a large, busy, and beautiful city.

7. The Rocky Mountains make a great dividing wall, extending across the entire country. Even the water from the springs on the eastern side goes away to the Mississippi, and finally to the *Atlantic* Ocean; while that on the western side flows to the *Pacific*. As you become older, you will be able to understand, much better than you now can, how very important this mountain system is.

XVII.—ON THE TABLE-LAND.

Si-er'-ra Ne-va'-da. | cañ'-on. | Co-lo-ra'-do [-rah'-].
[Si-er'-ra Ne-vah'-da]. | [can'-yon]. | pla-teau' [pla-to'].

1. BEYOND the Rocky Mountains, is another vast plain, many hundred miles broad; and on the western border of that, is another great system of mountains, called the *Sierra Nevada*. This whole plain between the two mountain systems is lifted up, so that it is higher than the ranges of the Appalachian Mountains.

ON THE TABLE-LAND. 67

Such a high plain is called a *table-land*, or sometimes a *plateau*.

2. On a large part of this great table-land, it rains but very few times in the year. For this reason, the soil is so dry that only a few kinds of plants can grow, and there are no forests. The low plants do not look fresh and green, but gray and dusty, so that, a little way from them, you would think you were looking only on the bare gray earth. You may travel for days, and find still the same dry, dreary country. How very different is this from the great forests of the Atlantic Plain, and the rich green prairies near the Mississippi!

3. Have you ever seen those plants called the *cactus* and the *prickly pear?* We have them set in boxes in our gardens;

The Cactus.

and in winter we keep them in a warm room. In a part of the table-land south of the middle, these are almost the only plants; and they grow much taller and larger than any we have, for that is their native country.

4. They are not covered with leaves, but are only great, branching, juicy stalks, with little bunches of hairs dotting them all over. These gather every bit of moisture there is in the air, and store it away in the great soft stalks; thus the cactus can grow where grasses and other plants would soon dry up and die. Many of them have large scarlet or crimson flowers, which are very beautiful.

5. In the hollows in different parts of the table-land, are lakes of salt water, some so salt that fish cannot live in them. Into some, little streams of water flow from the springs among the mountains and hills; and along the borders of these, you will find a line of fresh green grass, and sometimes trees. These green belts with the bright streams, in the midst of this broad, gray, dreary land, are very beautiful. They are almost the only places on the great table-land which are naturally productive. The largest of the lakes is *Great Salt Lake*. Near it, in the State of *Utah*, is a large, thriving city named after the lake, *Salt Lake City*.

6. In the whole table-land, where there is so little rain, there are but few rivers. These do not, like others which we have seen, flow through beautiful green valleys, with gentle slopes on each side, covered with farms and gardens. You may be riding across the country, and before you, as far as the eye can reach, there is no valley, no stream, to be seen.

7. Presently you look down, and right there under your feet, is a great crack in the earth, with a solid wall of rock, like the Palisades, on each side of it. Down as far as you can see, there is not a spot on which you could set your foot. At the bottom is a river, looking

ON THE TABLE-LAND. 69

Grand Cañon of the Colorado.

black and terrible in the dark shadow of the rocky walls. Such a place is called a *cañon*.

8. There are cañons on some part of the course of nearly all the larger streams. The *Colorado*, the largest river in all this part of the country, flows in deep cañons through almost its whole course.

9. You see that the country west of the Rocky Moun-

tains, is not a good land for farmers, for in most of it nothing useful can grow; and as the larger rivers flow through deep cañons, instead of fertile valleys, there are not many good places for cities. You would suppose people here could find nothing to do, and would have nothing to live on. But this is not so. In the mountains on the table-land, as well as in the Rocky Mountains, there are veins of gold and silver. Thus even this part of our country is good for something.

10. Men go to the mines to dig the gold and silver from the earth; others go to sell food and clothing to the miners; and so, after a time, a large number of people gather, and villages or cities spring up where we would not have supposed anybody could possibly live. These places are not very pleasant to live in. Some are far from any railroad; and most of the food for the people must be brought, with great difficulty, over this wild, dreary country, in wagons, or on the backs of mules traveling in long trains.

XVIII. — IN CALIFORNIA.

| Cal-i-for'-ni-a. | San Fran-cis'-co. | Los An'-gel-es. |
| ran-che'-ro [-cha'-]. | vine'-yard [vin'-]. | [Loce An'-hel-ez]. |

1. WHEN we have passed over the great table-land, we reach *California*, a part of our country of which, I have no doubt, you have often heard. It has, in the central part, the high wall of the Sierra Nevada, with peaks reaching up into the clouds and covered with snow and ice.

2. These snowy peaks shut in many narrow valleys, the sides of which are not gentle slopes, but steep precipices. Into some of them, rivers leap, forming waterfalls of immense height. West of this mountain border, is a wide and beautiful valley, with clear lakes and bright rivers that do not have their waters locked with ice in winter; for it is always warm there. Beyond this valley, is a range of low mountains like the Appalachians, and then comes the broad Pacific Ocean.

3. In the valleys of California are farms with great fields of grain, and orchards in which grow the most excellent fruits. There are also gardens of grapevines, called *vineyards*, much finer than those on the banks of the Ohio River. Many of the things that are raised on the farms or in the gardens of the East, grow in California much better and larger; besides, in parts of the State, are figs and oranges, and many other fruits that grow only in warm countries.

4. In the southern part of the State, there are large prairies, covered with tall, rich grass and wild oats, where thousands of cattle and horses are raised. Sometimes one man owns as much as a whole county. His land is not called a farm, but a *ranch*. Nobody, not even he himself, knows how many horses and cattle he has; for they run wild on the ranch. There are herdsmen, called *rancheros*, who have charge of them, but who really give them little attention.

5. Once a year the cattle are driven together and counted, and the young ones are marked so that they can be known; and that is about all the care they receive. As snow hardly ever lies on the ground, they feed all winter in the fields, upon the ripened oats and

the grass which has turned into hay while standing in the field.

6. In the valleys among the mountains of California, are forests of wonderful old trees, so large that you can hardly imagine how big they are. In several places, there are groves in which some trees are so large round that they would fill your whole schoolroom, and are twice as tall as the very tallest church steeple you ever saw. Nobody knows how long they have been growing; but they must have been there many hundred years before any white people came to this country.

The Bottom of One of the Big Trees.

7. But it was not the farms, nor ranches, nor forests, which first interested people in California. It was the great quantity of gold found in the mountains in the eastern part, which brought people here from every part of the world.

8. One day in the year 1848, when our people were just beginning to go there, and we knew hardly anything about it, a man who was at work near one of the streams flowing from these mountains found

some grains of gold in the sand which the water had washed down. This showed that there must be gold in the mountains from which the river came; and, as soon as it was heard of, thousands of people rushed to California to get rich.

9. At first everybody went to the gold fields. There were no farms bought and worked by the newcomers, no mills built, nor anything done but to dig for gold. For this reason, though this State has some of the best farming land in the world, and some of the finest forests, and can produce almost everything that people need, it then furnished them no supplies. The food for all those thousands of people, the cloth for their clothing, their boots and shoes, the spades and wheelbarrows they used in the mines, and even the timbers for their houses, all ready to be put together, — were sent there from the great cities of the Atlantic Plain, — New York, Philadelphia, and Boston.

10. But people soon found that they could become rich just as rapidly by buying farms and raising food for the miners, and building mills and making the things that were needed, as by working at the mines. Now there is much more grain, fruit, lumber, wine, butter, and cheese produced in California, than the people need for their own use; and they are able to send these things to other countries.

11. On one part of the seashore, the Pacific sends a long arm, like a great river or lake, far into the land. This is *San Francisco Bay*. The entrance from the ocean is between high, rocky walls, where the mountain range that borders the seashore, has been broken down to its foot. This entrance is the *Golden Gate*.

12. Beside this broad, blue, quiet bay, just within the Golden Gate, there stood, when the first gold seekers went to California, a small, ill-looking village. Most of the houses were made of a kind of clay or mud; the streets were narrow and dirty; and the people looked no more attractive than the town. On all this beautiful bay, only a few small vessels and a dozen or two fishing boats, could be seen.

13. Now, instead of this mean village, we find a great and rich city. Large, fine buildings adorn it; its streets are full of people hurrying to and fro; and the bay is covered with ships from every part of the world. This is one thing that has been done for California by the discovery of gold. The city which has grown up so quickly is *San Francisco*.

14. There are other fine cities now in all parts of the wide valley. On the southern coast, is a place where the country was so beautiful, and the air so delightful, that the people who discovered the site chose it at once for their dwelling place, and called the town they founded *Los Angeles*, which means "city of the angels."

15. The hillsides and valleys about the city are covered with vineyards, orange groves, and orchards, from which are sent out great quantities of delicious peaches, pears, figs, oranges, and grapes. They go not only to San Francisco and other parts of California, but even to New York, Philadelphia, and Boston.

16. For a time the Golden Gate was the only way of entrance to California, except the long weary journey by teams, across the great table-land. But now railroads lead from San Francisco, through all the principal cities, to every part of the country east of the Mississippi.

XIX.—IN THE NORTHWEST.

Mon-ta'-na [-*tah'*-]. | **Hel'-e-na.** | **Wy-o'-ming.**

1. IN California we touch the most southwestern part of our country, which borders upon the Pacific Ocean. The most northwestern part, in which are some very remarkable regions, also borders upon the Pacific. *Washington* and *Oregon*, together with *California*, occupy our entire Pacific coast.

2. To see this northern belt, we shall start from the middle portion of *Minnesota*, in which are the sources of the Mississippi, and travel westward, across the broadest part of the Rocky Mountain region. There are several lines of railroad by which we may go.

3. On the west of Minnesota lie two great States, *North Dakota* and *South Dakota*. The railroad by which we travel crosses the former. Here we pass rich, rolling prairies, and the ground is occupied by wheat farms of vast extent, yielding abundant harvests.

4. Farther westward the appearance of the country changes. The ground is higher, and, instead of wheat fields only, we begin to see rich pastures, where herds of cattle, sheep, and other animals are feeding. On and on we go, crossing the great Missouri River at *Bismarck*, the capital of the State; and continuing westward, we find ourselves at length in *Montana*.

5. By and by the surface becomes broken by low mountains, and we reach the Yellowstone River. The track of the railroad creeps carefully along its course, until we find a branch road leading directly southward

into the very heart of the Rocky Mountains, to that wonderful region, the *Yellowstone Park*. This lies mostly in *Wyoming*, the State next south of Montana; but the northern borders are in the latter State.

6. There, in 1872, a district nearly as large as Connecticut, was set apart by our government, to be a *National Park*, because of its remarkable natural features. There are high mountains, cataracts, deep gorges, or cañons, through which large streams flow, and hot springs and basins called *geysers*, which now and then spout columns of hot water high into the air.

7. Our railroad still keeps its westward course, but presently turns northward, carrying us into the most mountainous portion of Montana. This part of the State is rich in copper, gold, silver, and other metals; and mining towns and cities have grown up in the wildest and roughest parts. Now that railroads have been built, connecting these with the more thickly settled portions, many of the towns are growing rapidly. *Helena* is the capital of Montana.

8. From Helena, the road passes on, among high mountains, between ranges, and across difficult passes, until, when not far from the northern boundary of the United States, it descends into a less wild region, and crosses *Idaho* into northern Washington. Idaho thus lies next west of the States of Montana and Wyoming, and shares in the abundance of valuable metals found in the ranges of the Rocky Mountains.

9. Great numbers of streams, that rise in the high ranges of eastern Idaho, pass westward into the lower lands, their courses interrupted by rapids and falls, so that they are not navigable. At length all unite to

form the *Columbia River*, which, having found a pathway down the *Cascade Mountains* and through the *Coast Ranges*, enters the Pacific Ocean. The course of the main stream separates Washington from Oregon.

10. Idaho and the eastern half of Washington and Oregon occupy the northern part of that great interior table-land that we crossed in Utah and found so barren. But here the great mountain ranges north of the Sierra Nevada are less high and are much broken, and they allow warm winds, laden with moisture, to sweep over them far into the interior. Hence there is abundance of rain, and the soil is productive.

11. In northwestern Washington, a wide break through the Coast Ranges lets the water of the ocean flow into the inner valley, and the lowest lands are covered. Thus is formed *Puget Sound*, full of beautiful forest-covered islands. There are many large bays and excellent harbors, along which are busy towns and cities. In Oregon, instead of bays and harbors, with fine sites for cities, the valley is drained by the *Willamette River*, and the largest cities are along its course. Extensive forests of pine and cedar cover vast areas. West of the Cascade Mountains, in particular, is one of the richest lumber districts in the United States.

12. In all this northern belt of States, the largest numbers of people are along the lines of railroad, opening to them the distant markets. The trains carry away not only metals, but vast quantities of wheat, cattle, and wool; for here, again, we begin to see vast wheat farms and grazing lands, such as we saw in North Dakota, but lost sight of when we entered the mining districts of Montana.

XX.—IN THE COLD COUNTRIES OF THE NORTH.

Do-min'-ion. | au-ro'-ra. | rein'-deer.

1. NORTH of the United States, there is a country much colder than ours. It, also, extends from the Atlantic to the Pacific Ocean: and it stretches northward to the shores of still another ocean, called the *Arctic*. This country, formerly called *British America*, is now named the *Dominion of Canada*.

2. The larger part of this cold region is one great forest, reaching nearly to the shores of the Arctic Ocean. In it are wild animals of many different kinds,—the wolf, bear, reindeer, moose, musk ox, and others.

A Reindeer.

3. Almost the only people in all this great forest are Indians, who spend their time in hunting and fishing. Here and there, by the side of some of the large lakes and rivers, are a few white men, who live there in order to hunt the wild animals for their furs, or to buy furs and skins from the Indian hunters. Some of the furs are sold to the people of Canada, but many are sent away to other cold countries. In all this forest country, during half the year or more, the ground is covered with snow and ice, and the rivers and lakes are frozen over.

IN THE COLD COUNTRIES OF THE NORTH.

4. Far to the north, the forest becomes thin and the trees very small. By and by there are no longer any trees. They cannot grow here, not because it is too dry, as was the case in the table-land west of the Rocky Mountains, but because *it is too cold*. There are only a few low shrubs; and near the shore of the Arctic Ocean, even these all disappear, and nothing grows but mosses, and other low plants.

5. Here the snow is on the ground all the year except a month or two; and even then, if you should dig into the earth a little way, you would find it frozen. When the snow is gone, the sun warms the surface; and the plants quickly spring up, blossom, and bear their fruits. The reindeer and musk ox come from the forest to feed on the fresh mosses; and for a short time, this cold, dreary region seems quite bright.

A Musk Ox.

6. On the Arctic shores, as you see, the summer lasts only about a month. All the rest of the year is winter; and, what will seem strange to you, the winter days are very, *very* short. Just before Christmas, there is one day in which the sun does not rise at all, and there are two or three weeks in which you hardly see it. It is night nearly all the time, but not very dark, for the stars are bright; and the white snow and the large moon shining brightly, make the night nearly as light as the day. These, with the brilliant northern lights,

or *aurora*, in the sky, make the long winter nights much more pleasant than we would suppose.

7. After a winter night, which lasts as long as from noon to-day until noon to-morrow, there is, about twelve o'clock, a brightness in the southern horizon, like that which we see in the east just before the sun rises. This continues only a short time; but these few minutes of dim light are the whole of the shortest winter day.

8. The next day, about twelve o'clock, the sun peeps above the southern horizon for a half hour, and then goes away again. The next day he stays a little longer, rising earlier, and setting later; and so on, each day, until, in June, there is one day in which he does not set, and several days in which he shines nearly all the time, hardly disappearing at all. Thus you see, throughout the year, there is no more night than day, just as it is everywhere. But when the sun is up, it does not give much warmth, for it never rises high in the heavens, but moves around upon the horizon, toward the north at midnight, and toward the south at noon.

9. You know that the sun rises in the east, goes through the southern sky, and sets in the west. We see it on only three sides of us. But in the Arctic regions, in that longest day in summer, the sun goes quite round the heavens, and may be seen on the horizon directly in the north. Is not that very singular? Many people who live there, I suppose, think that it is just the same all over the earth.

10. A very singular people, called Eskimos, live about the Arctic Ocean. Though the country is so cold that we should hardly suppose any one could live there, they seem to make themselves very comfortable.

11. Their clothing is made from the skins of wild animals, especially from that of the reindeer. They prepare it with the hair on, and make a sort of dress all in one piece, — cap, shirt, trousers, and shoes. Their chief food is fish and the flesh of the reindeer, and of the seal, walrus, and whale, which inhabit the icy seas.

12. The reindeer stays here only during the short summer, while it can obtain food; so the people must kill enough then to last them all the year. The women cut up the meat, and dry it, and in this way keep it for the long winter. They also catch and dry the fish.

13. Through the winter, the Eskimos live in log huts, which they build from the trunks of trees that have floated down the long rivers from the forests. They pile up snow around and over the hut, and make a hole in one side, at the bottom, through which they creep in and out. Here they stay from the time when the leaves of our trees begin to fall, until they are green again in spring. Then all quit their winter quarters, and go to the islands along the coast to watch for the seal. There they build houses of snow.

Eskimo Girl.

14. The Arctic Ocean is full of ice in summer as well as in winter. The wind drives it from one place to another, and sometimes great masses, called *icebergs*, strike against ships and dash them to pieces.

An Iceberg.

XXI.—IN THE WARM COUNTRIES OF THE SOUTH.

West In′-dies. | Mon-te-zu′-ma [-zoo′-]. | dah′-lia [*dah′-lya*].

1. SOUTH of the United States are the warm countries of *Mexico* and *Central America,* and some great islands, called the *West Indies,* which lie in the adjacent ocean. There the whole year is one constant summer.

2. In crossing Mexico from east to west, there is first a broad plain by the seaside, covered with immense forests. Here grows the tall, beautiful *cocoa palm*, straight as an arrow, and covered with a crown of long

green, feathery leaves, under which are the large clusters of fruit. The *mahogany*, from the wood of which furniture is made, and the *banana* and other plants yielding delicious fruits, are also found here.

3. By and by we begin to ascend a slope, many parts of which are so steep and rugged that the roads are very narrow, crooked, and often dangerous. Here, too, are fine forests, also plantations of cotton, coffee, and tobacco. Lovely *roses*, *dahlias*, and many other plants grow here in the fields and forests.

4. At length we find ourselves on the top of a mountain range, which we cross and descend into a basin, or plain, surrounded by mountains. This inclosed plain is the *table-land of Mexico*. In the midst of it, is a beautiful lake, beside which is the famous old city of *Mexico*.

5. When the white people first came to America, over four hundred years ago, they found the lake much larger than it now is, and the city on a cluster of islands in the midst of the lake. A powerful king, named Montezuma, lived here with his people, who were called *Aztecs*. The city was full of their palaces and temples, many of which were ornamented with figures and vessels of silver and gold, and with wonderful carvings and paintings.

6. They had lived for three hundred years in this basin, with its high mountains on all sides, shutting them in away from the warlike Indians beyond, who never thought of doing anything but to hunt and fight. They were thus able to go on in peace, building their palaces, temples, bridges, and other great works, some of which were very remarkable. But what seemed most wonderful to the white strangers, was the great

number of articles of silver and gold in the temples and palaces. These they wanted; and they wished also to know where the silver and gold were obtained, so that they might get them for themselves. As the king would not tell them this, they took him prisoner, and afterward made war on the city, and treated his people very cruelly.

7. In the war, the city was nearly destroyed; but it was soon rebuilt by the conquerors. They finally found the mines which had been worked by the natives; and soon great numbers of white people came there to live. But they cared more for the gold and silver than for anything else in Mexico.

8. *Central America*, which is farther south, resembles Mexico very much, except that it is even warmer. It has more rain too; and the choice trees, fruits, and flowers of that country grow still more luxuriantly here.

9. In both Mexico and Central America, there are mountains like chimneys, through which melted rock, cinders, and vapor come out from the interior of the earth. These mountains are called *volcanoes*. Sometimes there come out from volcanoes such great quantities of cinders, that cities and villages near them are buried. Sometimes, also, red-hot streams of melted rock, called *lava*, flow down the mountain side, burning up everything in their way.

10. At times, noises like thunder are heard within the earth; and the solid land trembles, so that the houses are shaken like boats on the sea, and come tumbling down over the heads of the frightened people. This trembling of the earth is called an *earthquake*.

IN THE WARM COUNTRIES OF THE SOUTH. 85

Earthquakes not only happen in Mexico and Central America, but also in other countries. Sometimes they shake down whole cities, and open great chasms in the earth, swallowing up both animals and people.

11. We find that the United States is in the middle of a very great body of land, the northern part of which is frozen throughout the year; while the southern part has, all the year long, one constant summer. This vast body of land is called a *continent*, and the name of it is *North America*. Our country, though so very large, is much less than one half of it.

12. There are five other continents upon the earth, two of which are much larger than North America. Yet we know that there is about three times as much water as land on the earth's surface. What a great earth it is on which we live, and how many beautiful things we have already seen in it! We shall find many more when we go to the other continents, as we shall do by and by.

A Volcano.

XXII.—THE WEST INDIES.

Ha-van'-a. | ve-ran'-da. | ba-na'-na [-*ah'-nah*].

1. THESE islands lie in the ocean, east of the Gulf of Mexico. Four of them are much larger than the others. They are covered with rugged mountains, among which are broad green valleys where not a flake of snow ever falls, nor a particle of ice is formed.

2. The forests are filled with large trees, that bear fresh green leaves, flowers, and fruits throughout the year, as in the lowlands of Mexico and Central America. The earth beneath the trees is covered with beautiful feathery ferns, lovely flowers, and many singular plants.

3. Suppose you are traveling in the forests, and become thirsty. You look about for a spring or brook of cool, pure water, from which to drink. You may not find any, because sometimes no rain falls for several months, and the springs and brooks become quite dry.

4. Here beside you, climbing from tree to tree, is a vine that looks as much like a dead grapevine as anything can. As high up as you can reach, you cut a notch in a branch of it, and lower down you cut the branch entirely off. Putting the end to your mouth, you suck upon it, and find that it gives you a small stream of delicious cool water, which it has drawn up from the earth, and stored away to feed the plant in this dry time. There are many other plants that thus provide water for themselves. What a happy thing to find such plants in this warm, and sometimes very dry, country!

5. In all the large islands, especially in *Cuba*, are great plantations of *sugar cane*, *coffee*, and *tobacco*. The city of *Havana*, on the northern coast of this island, is one of the greatest sugar markets in the world.

A Sugar Plantation.

6. The sugar plantations are everywhere much alike. In some pleasant part the owner lives in a large, low house, with broad verandas on every side, and palm trees shading it. Around it grow clusters of orange trees, bananas, and other fruit-bearing plants.

7. Not far away is the great sugar mill, in which the cane is crushed, and its juice pressed out and made into sugar and molasses. Near by it stands a large cluster of little cabins. Each has a banana plant and a small garden beside it; and groups of naked negro children are seen rolling about in the dust, or lying asleep in the sunshine. These are the houses of the negroes, who do all the work of raising the cane, and making the sugar.

8. On every side of this little village the vast cane field extends, so that you might ride for miles and still find it everywhere the same. You would pass none of the small, neat farmhouses you are accustomed to see; but after a time would find another plantation just like the last, with its great house, its mill, and its little cabins clustered together in the midst of the cane fields.

9. The white people on all these islands do but little work. They usually stay in their houses through the warmest part of the day; and when the sun goes down they go out to ride, make visits, and amuse themselves as they choose.

SOUTH AMERICA.

I.—UP THE AMAZON.

Pa-na-ma' [-mah']. | Ma-ra-jo' [-zho']. | Pa-ra' [Pah-rah'].

1. SOUTHWARD from North America is *South America*. Like North America, it lies between the Atlantic Ocean and the Pacific. These two continents are connected by a narrow neck of land, named the *Isthmus of Panama*.

2. In the northern part of South America is an immense river, the largest in the world. Its source is in the far western part of the continent, near the Pacific Ocean. It flows eastward more than three thousand miles, through a vast, low plain, into the Atlantic. This is the *Amazon* River.

3. The mouth of the Amazon is so broad as to seem like a large lake; and its great mass of muddy, yellow water can be seen for many miles at sea, making its way through the clear blue ocean. Just at the mouth of the river is the large island of *Marajo*, dividing the stream into two branches,— one more than twenty miles wide, the other more than fifty. This island is covered with pastures and plantations, from which are sent cattle, rice, sugar, and fruits. On the banks of the Amazon, south of Marajo, is the city of *Para*.

4. Like New Orleans, it is built on the marshy plains that border the river, and is surrounded by rice fields and sugar plantations. It is now only a small place, but some day it will undoubtedly become a large and busy city; for steamers can go from Para up the Amazon and its great tributaries to all parts of the interior of South America, just as they go from New Orleans up the Mississippi to the interior of our own country.

5. After having traveled by steamer up the Amazon, from Para, for a day or two, all the plantations disappear, and we see along the river only immense marshes. They are covered with a thick growth of reeds, often much higher than a common house. Here and there are open spaces, where the water is covered with large, round green leaves, that, with their brown edges turning upward,

On the Amazon.

look like flatboats. Some of them are as many as six feet across; and, if you were placed in the middle of one, you would find it quite strong enough to support you on the water.

6. These are the leaves of the beautiful *Victoria Regia*, a very large kind of water lily. Floating on the water, among these great leaves, are flowers larger than a common dinner plate. The inner petals are of a pretty rose color, and in the center is a circle of bright gold; while the rest of the flower is snowy white. You can

Victoria Regia.

hardly imagine one more beautiful. These, and the many other plants growing there, make the marshes of the Amazon very wonderful to see.

7. But among all these pleasant things, there are others which you will not like so well. Great scaly alligators lie asleep in the sunshine, with their ugly red mouths wide open, or float like logs on the surface of the water; immense water snakes glide about among the reeds; large frogs and turtles and lizards are to be seen at every moment; and the air is filled with the hum of brilliant insects whose sting is poisonous.

8. Here and there long-legged swamp birds wade about, darting their long beaks into the water after the frogs and snakes, which they devour; while whole

flocks, which have finished their fishing, stand asleep on the shore. The noonday sun, directly over our heads, pours down his burning rays, and almost blinds us by the dazzling light that is reflected from the water.

9. All the morning the whole sky has been perfectly clear and of the brightest blue. Now banks of white clouds are piled up here and there. They grow thick and dark, and rapidly become larger; and soon the whole sky is black. The lightning darts in blinding

An Alligator.

flashes from one side of the heavens to the other. Terrible peals of thunder shake the earth, and the rain begins to fall in torrents. This continues until near night; then the thunder, lightning, and rain cease, the clouds disappear, and all night the heavens are bright with stars.

10. Every day for several weeks is just the same; only that each day the rain commences a little earlier, and ceases later, than the day before, until at length it rains all day. Then it begins later and later each day, and ceases earlier; and at last there comes a time during

which, for a number of months, no rain falls. The part of the year in which it rains thus each day is called the *wet season;* the other part, the *dry season.* They are nearly alike in heat, for the larger part of South America has no winter.

II.—IN THE SILVAS.

| sil'-va. | ja-guar'. | Ri'-o [*Re'-*] de Ja-ne-i'-ro [-*na'-*]. |
| bo'-a con-stric'-tor. | Bra-zil'. | va-nil'-la. |

1. BEYOND the marshes which border the stream on each side, are immense forests, stretching away hundreds of miles. The trees are not only of great size, but they stand so close together that their branches are interlocked and form a dense roof of green, through which the sunbeams can hardly reach the earth.

2. The whole space between the trees, and beneath their branches, is one mass of reeds and other tall plants. Thousands of vines climb about them, stretching from tree to tree and hanging down from the branches, thus binding all so firmly together that, in some places, not even a footpath can be made through the forests without an ax to cut the way.

3. The low plants, the vines, and even many of the great trees, are covered with the most beautiful flowers, not only white, but crimson, purple, scarlet, and golden yellow. As there is no winter, the trees are at all times growing, blooming, and bearing fruit. On some kinds, buds, flowers, green fruit, and ripened fruit may be found all at the same time.

4. Living among the branches of the trees, are multi-

tudes of birds, of such brilliant colors that they seem like winged flowers. Numberless *monkeys* of every description, some of which are not larger than a kitten, chase each other from tree to tree, swinging by their long tails from one branch to another. Great snakes, called *boa constrictors*, some of them eight or ten yards in length, hang from the trees, watching for some animal to come within their reach, when they quickly wind themselves round him, and crush him.

5. Still another terrible creature, called the *jaguar*, makes his home in the forests. The young ones look like kittens, and, playing about the trees, are very pretty and harmless; but when grown large they are fierce and dangerous. Thousands of animals of many other kinds fill this great forest, through which the rivers are almost the only paths, and where few people but Indians and adventurous travelers have ever been.

Spider Monkeys.

6. Although there are such vast numbers of birds and animals here, the forests, all through the long, warm days, are perfectly silent. There is not a sound of bird or beast; but as soon as the night comes on their voices are everywhere heard. The roaring of the fierce and angry jaguar, the screaming of the frightened monkeys trying to escape, the chattering of the parrots and other birds which have been wakened by the noise, make a sort of music that is not very charming, and which, I think, would hardly lull one to sleep.

7. Travelers who may be obliged to spend the night in the forests must build fires all about them to keep away the jaguars and other dangerous animals. They are afraid of the flame, and will not approach it. But for this, it would not be safe for any one to go to sleep in the forests. These broad plains, through which the Amazon and its tributaries flow, are called *silvas*, which means *forest plains*.

8. We steam up the Amazon, day after day, for more than a month, and still we find a wide level plain covered with the same forests. Were we to leave the main stream and go up any one of its many large tributaries, we should find no change; for the silvas cover more than half the continent of South America. The great variety of trees mingled together in the same forest, with no one kind especially noticeable, seems surprising to us, because in our country we often see vast forests of only a single kind, as pine, birch, or maple. Many of the large trees bear bright flowers.

9. Far away to the west the country through which the Amazon flows becomes hilly; and at length the river, now much smaller, descends, in many rapids and

waterfalls, from a mountainous region. The **forests** begin to be broken, and plantations and villages again appear. Here we must leave the river, as steamers can go no farther.

10. The silvas form a large part of a great country named *Brazil*, which is nearly as large as all the other countries of South America. But the southeastern part is a table-land, with low mountains crossing it in every direction. In these mountains, and among the pebbles of the streams that flow from them, gold and diamonds are found.

11. In the southeastern part of Brazil are many coffee plantations, orange groves, and gardens of bananas and pineapples. These, with cotton, tobacco, rice, and other things which grow in the warm parts of our own country, may be raised in all the rich valleys. There is also growing here a vine that bears a fruit like a bean, from which a delicious perfume is obtained. This is the *vanilla*. Many of you have seen either the **vanilla** bean, or an extract made from it.

Picking Coffee.

12. But there are not yet half enough white **people** in Brazil to cultivate all its rich land. Almost the

only inhabitants of the interior are Indians, who live upon the fruits of the forest. With them are missionaries who are trying to teach them.

13. On the coast is the large city of *Rio de Janeiro.* Its streets are shaded by palms and other beautiful trees. In some places the handsome buildings, of which there are many, are almost hidden by the green leaves. The air, too, is always delightful, much like that of Los Angeles, in California.

14. The city is built by the side of a broad blue bay, dotted with lovely islands; and behind it rise green hills, and high, forest-covered mountains. These hills are topped with pleasant country houses half hidden by trees; and the rich valleys between them are covered with fields of coffee, cotton, sugar, and delicious pineapples. Rio de Janeiro and *Santos* (another city of Brazil) are the greatest coffee markets in the world.

III.—ACROSS THE ANDES.

An′-des. | **lla′-ma** [*lah′-ma*]. | **ca-ca′-o** [*ka*].

1. THE mountains from which the Amazon flows, and at the foot of which the steamers stop, are the *Andes.* They are very high, and form a continuous elevation along the western coast, from the northern point of South America to the southern. Nowhere can we go from the Atlantic Ocean to the Pacific without crossing the Andes.

2. We left the Amazon just at the foot of the mountains. We shall continue our journey on the back of

a mule, for there are no good roads over the Andes. Their slopes are so rough and broken, that it is very difficult and dangerous to travel across them. Sometimes the way lies along the edge of a precipice, where the path is only wide enough for the mule to walk. A

Among the Andes.

single wrong step would throw us down hundreds of feet, and we should be dashed in pieces.

3. In other places, we pass through deep gorges, with perpendicular rocks on each side, rising far above; and we are continually in danger of being crushed by falling pieces. Foaming mountain streams at the bottom of deep ravines must be crossed, not on solid stone bridges, but on slender, swinging cords, covered only with branches of trees, ready to break at any moment, and plunge us into the terrible chasm below. Across

some of the least difficult passes, lines of railroad have of late been constructed, so that the towns in the high valleys can have much more intercourse with the low lands than used to be possible.

4. On the lower parts of the slope, are dense forests, like those of the silvas, with the same kinds of trees and animals. Farther up the mountain we find no more tall palm trees, nor trees covered with brilliant flowers; but instead, beautiful maples, oaks, and elms, such as we see in our own country.

5. At the foot of the Andes the whole year is one long, warm summer. Higher up, it is like constant spring. The sunny blue sky is always smiling; and the pleasant valleys among the mountains are filled with grainfields, green pastures, and pretty villages.

6. Still higher we reach a cold country, with but a few stunted trees, somewhat like those growing near the Arctic shores of North America. Now we are at the top of the great wall of the Andes; and here, spread out before us, is a bare, rocky plain, cold, gray, and very dreary. Only a few dwarfed shrubs, grasses, and other poor, starved-looking plants, cover the earth. Away in the distance, against the dark-blue sky, rising far above us, are cone-shaped peaks, covered nearly from top to bottom with mantles of snow, and shining in the sunlight like silver mountains. Many of these are volcanic, and they are all very high.

7. Here and there, all over this dreary plain, are little villages, with herds of *llamas* feeding on the scanty pastures. The llamas are natives of these cold heights, and were once found wild in great numbers. They have been tamed, and are now used by the people of

the Andes to carry goods up and down the dangerous slopes. They are very useful; because, though quite small and slow, they are gentle. They are also perfectly sure-footed, never stumbling nor slipping on the most difficult mountain paths, where hardly any other animal can travel.

8. After we have crossed the summit of this great range, we descend into a beautiful, high valley, beyond which is another range, as high and as rugged as the first one. In this valley, with the high mountain walls and the snowy volcanoes shutting it in on every side, we find again constant spring. The earth is adorned with forests, grainfields, orchards, and gardens, in the midst of which are bright rivers, blue lakes, villages, and great cities.

9. Here, long ago, lived a people resembling those who built cities on the table-land of Mexico. All the inner valleys of the Andes were full of their cities and temples, rich in gold and silver; while broad, fine roads led from one valley to another. These cities, like those of Mexico, were finally found by the white men. The people were conquered, and their noble works destroyed by the conquerors, who cared only for their gold and silver. Finally the mines were discovered, and the cities were rebuilt by the new inhabitants.

10. Among the trees of these valleys, is a beautiful one called the *cacao*. It is somewhat like the cherry tree in size and form, and bears a fruit containing a number of oily kernels. From these kernels is prepared the delicious chocolate, so much used upon our tables.

11. Another tree, very precious to the people, **grows** in some of the warmest of the valleys. It is the *cow*

tree.. When the bark is cut, there flows out from it an abundant juice, white and a little gummy, with a very pleasant taste and smell. It flows most freely about sunrise. Then you may see Indians and negroes coming from all directions to the trees, with large vases or jugs which they fill with this sort of milk. They are very fond of it, and it makes a good food.

12. The highest of the inner valleys are cold and dreary, like the plains on the summit of the range; but even some of these have mining cities, and the food for the thousands of people who live and work there is nearly all brought by the llamas from the warm, fruitful valleys below.

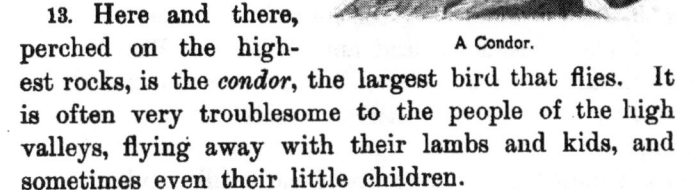

A Condor.

13. Here and there, perched on the highest rocks, is the *condor*, the largest bird that flies. It is often very troublesome to the people of the high valleys, flying away with their lambs and kids, and sometimes even their little children.

14. The second range is just as difficult to cross as the first one. Descending it to the foot of the mountains, we reach a region where there is little rain, and where, although it is warm, there is little vegetation. And now we come at once to the shore of the great Pacific; for the Andes lie close along the western border of the continent.

IV.—ON THE LLANOS.

lla'-nos [*lah'-*]. | las'-so. | O-ri-no'-co.

1. NORTH of the Amazon is another great river, also flowing from a mountain country through a vast plain, northeastward, into the Atlantic. This is the *Orinoco*. The plains of the Orinoco, like those of the Amazon, are quite level. Nowhere can a hill of any size be seen, but here and there a sort of table of naked rock rises up above the level surface of the ground.

2. Along the banks of the river, and on the rocky islands in the midst of it, are dense forests, like those which border the Amazon; but elsewhere, all over the great plain, not a tree can be seen. These treeless plains are called *llanos*, meaning *open plains*.

3. Through the llanos, at the end of the dry season, the river winds between low, flat banks, everywhere fringed with narrow bands of green forests or grasses. All the vast plain beside is dead and desolate. The earth is black and dry; and the hot sun pours down upon it, without even a cloud between to shield it from the burning rays.

4. Now the rains begin. Torrents of water fall; and in a few days the river fills up, and overflows its banks. Grass and flowers spring up all over the plains; and in a short time the wide llanos are carpeted with green, dotted with gold, crimson, purple, and every brilliant color.

5. Herds of wild horses and cattle pasture upon the rich grass, which is soon tall enough to hide them from

view; or dash over the plains, pursued by swift riders, who catch them with a long rope fastened firmly to the saddle. This rope is called a *lasso*. It is wound into a ring, or coil, and held in the right hand; and, when the rider is near enough to the animal he wishes to catch, he throws it with all his might. He is so skill-

Lassoing Cattle.

ful, that, as the coil unwinds, a noose at its end is sure to fall around the horns or head of the animal, so that it cannot escape. Now the horse holds himself firmly braced, and lets the poor beast pull at the lasso until it is tired out, when it is drawn up and secured.

6. The air is filled with insects; and the moist earth swarms with snakes, lizards, frogs, and turtles. Great

alligators watch by the river side for the animals that come down to drink; and the jaguar, from the forest, comes here to prey upon the herds which feed on these rich pastures.

7. By and by the rainy season is over, and the sun pours down again its burning heat. After a few weeks, the river shrinks away to its former size, all the little pools and streams that were formed over the plain are gone. At length the earth is dry and hard, and cracked in every direction; and the beautiful green grass has become yellow and dried everywhere, except close along the borders of the river. The dry, hot wind raises thick clouds of dust, and makes the air seem warmer instead of cooler. The red, dazzling sunlight nearly blinds you, and the heat makes you weak and sick.

8. Now you do not see any frogs or snakes; for they know when the dry season is coming, and bury themselves in the earth, to sleep until it is past, just as they do in our country during the winter. They do not like the very dry, hot weather any better than they do the cold. The swarms of insects are all dead; and the horses and the cattle are driven away to pastures near the mountains, for they would die without water. The whole plain is deserted and silent.

9. The herdsmen set fire to the dried grass in order to clear the ground for a new growth. Now the whole great plain, for hundreds of miles, is swept by the flames, everything is destroyed, and the earth is left black and bare, as we first saw it. This is one reason why no trees grow here. Every little one which may start during the wet season from seed scattered over the ground is killed by the drought and the fires each year.

V.—UP THE LA PLATA.

La Plá-ta. | Pa-ra-ná'. | Gau'-cho.
[Lah Pluh'-tah]. | [Pah-rah-nah']. | [Gow'-cho].
pam'-pas. | Gran Cha'-co [Chah'-]. | gal'-lop-ing [-lup-].

1. SOUTH of the Amazon is still another large river. Like the Mississippi, it gathers its waters from the mountain lands east and west of it, and flows southward through a great plain. Near the mouth it is called the *La Plata;* but the long stream above is named the *Parana.*

2. The plains of the La Plata, called *pampas*, are not like those of the Mississippi, nor like the silvas or the llanos. There are no great forests, nor rich prairies; but, instead, the ground is covered during the wet season with coarse grass growing two or three yards high, mixed with clover and thistles even higher. They are so large that they seem like young trees, more than like the plants of the same kind which we are accustomed to see.

3. In some places, are great forests of these tall, strong thistles, so dense that it is impossible to pass through them, except by the paths made by the herds of wild horses and cattle that feed upon the pampas. It is very dangerous to travel through these thickets; for robbers hide themselves beside the paths, and kill and rob those who come within their reach. For this reason there is little traveling across the pampas, except during the dry season, when the thistles are dead and burned, like the grasses of the llanos.

4. The inhabitants of the pampas are either Indians or a race of half-breeds, called *Gauchos*. The Gauchos are a half-wild people, spending almost their whole time on horseback, and riding the swiftest and wildest horses easily and safely. They sleep upon the ground, and are very proud of their wild, free life.

Pampas.

5. There were not always wild horses and cattle on the llanos and pampas. These plains were once covered with native animals, as the silvas now are. The white people brought the first horses and cattle from Europe; and these have increased in numbers so fast as to drive away nearly all the native animals.

6. Farther up the river, the pampas disappear; **and**

the plains through which the Parana flows are rich prairies, with timber along the streams. Here and there over the prairies, are low round hills covered with trees, looking like islands in the great sea of grass.

7. Toward the sources of the river, the woodlands increase, and there is only here and there a little, bright prairie smiling among their darker green. This is the *Gran Chaco*, or great hunting ground of the Indians; and they can be seen on their fleet horses, galloping over the prairies, gathering themselves together on the banks of the river, ready for the chase.

8. The ground here is so very level that there is scarcely a division between the tributaries of one great stream and those of another. In time of high water, it is possible to go by boat, across overflowed lands, from one to another. Thus, one may enter the La Plata, pass up the Parana and other tributaries northward, and cross over to the Madeira, the great tributary of the Amazon from the south. Near the mouth of the Madeira, a large tributary from the north enters the Amazon. By means of this, one can reach the Orinoco, and so descend to the ocean, crossing, by means of rivers, more than half the length of South America from south to north.

9. Some day we may see these streams bordered with cities, and covered with swift steamers bearing away the cotton, the coffee, and the sugar, which will then be growing where now are only forests and wild prairies. You know that it is not a great while since the cotton plantations and grain farms along the Mississippi were wild forests and prairies, with the Indians for their only inhabitants.

THE ATLANTIC OCEAN.

LIFE ON AND IN THE OCEAN.

New'-found-land. | con'-ti-nent. | har-poon'.

1. EAST of North and South America, you remember, is the Atlantic Ocean. Beyond the ocean, are two other continents, — Europe, which is opposite us; and Africa, opposite Mexico and South America. At the north, the Atlantic joins the frozen ocean called the *Arctic* Ocean, on the shores of which the Eskimos live; and at the south it joins another frozen ocean called the *Antarctic* Ocean. You see that those parts of it must be very cold; but the middle is warm, like the lands beside it.

2. In every part of this ocean, are ships going to and fro between the continents that border it, carrying goods and people from one country to another. Great steamers, also, built on purpose to carry passengers, are constantly plying between our large seaports, like New York and Boston, and the ports of Europe. They go as fast as possible all the time, — day and night; but the ocean is so very broad, that they are six to ten days in crossing it.

3. Before people began to build steamers, it took much longer to cross the Atlantic. The ships go scarcely half as fast as the steamers; and if there is

bad weather, they may be hindered so as to take a month or more for the voyage. In a calm, the great ships drift lazily, with their broad, drooping sails bathed in sunlight; but the steamers dash along at their usual rate, pouring into the air clouds of smoke, and raising a great foam and flurry along their path. Almost every new steamer that is put on, crosses the ocean in less

An Ocean Steamer leaving Port.

time than any before it; and travelers are becoming less and less anxious about the ocean trip.

4. Sometimes both ships and steamers set out with everything fair, and are never heard of afterward. Some take fire and are burned in mid ocean; others spring a leak and sink. Others still are driven by storms far out of their course, and injured so that they cannot get back; and finally they sink.

5. In crossing the Atlantic, we are for many days far from the sight of any land. All around us, is the great world of water, stretching away to the horizon, with perhaps not even a ship in view. The sun seems to come up out of the sea in the morning, and to sink into it at night. You would almost believe the ocean to be the whole world, and the people in the ship the only ones on its surface.

6. But the sea is full of life. In some places, are miles and miles of seaweed growing on the top of the water; in others, are immense schools of *dolphins* swimming for days beside the ship, sometimes darting almost out of the water, and making graceful curving lines at every motion. Timid little *flying fish* leap out into the air when they want to escape an enemy. Great flocks of sea birds sail about on the wing, or dive into the sea after fish, or float on the surface to rest.

7. But the most wonderful thing to see is the ocean itself, on a quiet night. Sometimes the ship leaves a path of light behind it, on the broad dark waters; and every little creature that plays on the surface is surrounded by a circle of light, making the ocean very brilliant. You see there are many things that even children can learn about the great ocean; but there are very many other things for you to learn by and by.

8. Besides the ships that transport passengers and goods, there are others which take men away to the cold parts of the ocean, to catch the whale. When a whale is seen, some of the sailors get into a small, strong boat, and row toward it. Fastened to the boat, are long, stout ropes, with sharp spears, called *harpoons*, attached to the ends. When the boat has come near

LIFE ON AND IN THE OCEAN.

enough, the master stands up, and throws a harpoon with all his force, and fixes it in the body of the whale.

9. He plunges down deep into the water, and the boatmen let the rope out longer and longer, so that the boat will not be drawn down too. They know he can-

Whale Fishing.

not stay under long, for he must come to the top to breathe. The master has other harpoons ready to strike him again when he comes up, until he is killed. But sometimes the angry whale strikes the boat, and breaks it to pieces; and then, without help, all the sailors might be drowned.

10. The body of the whale is now brought alongside the vessel, and fastened to it, so that it cannot float away. The men stand on the back, and cut off the fat, which is boiled in great kettles in order to get the oil. This is put into barrels to be carried home. The ship stays in the whale fields until it obtains a full cargo of oil, so the sailors are sometimes gone for three years.

11. There are vessels engaged in other kinds of fishery, in parts of the Atlantic. Opposite the mouth of the St. Lawrence, is a large island, called *Newfoundland*. Around this island, the sea is thronged with excellent fish; and hundreds, and sometimes thousands, of vessels, are occupied there during the season for fishing. The waters all along the coasts abound in excellent fish, and great numbers of little fishing vessels are flitting here and there in pursuit of them.

EUROPE.

I.—ENGLAND.—THE COUNTRY.

Eng′-land [*Ing′-land*].　|　**Ire′-land.**　|　**Scot′-land.**

1. NEAR the coast of Europe, in the Atlantic Ocean, are two great islands, named *Great Britain* and *Ireland*. Great Britain was once divided into three separate countries, — England, Scotland, and Wales. They are now all united in one, though people still use these names for the different parts of the island.

2. *England* is a lovely country. There you will find the pretty, neat farms separated by hedges instead of fences. There are hedges, too, skirting the roadsides and lanes; and the fields are fresh and green, as though the whole country were a carefully tended garden. Here and there, is a great house or castle, very large, old, and strong, though not always very attractive. In it live the rich people who own all the land for several miles around it. Their fathers and grandfathers have lived there before them, not quite ever since the world began, but for a very, very long time, and, therefore, they are fond and proud of their great old castles.

3. Around the castle, are beautiful parks, with fine large trees shading them, — elms and oaks and beeches,

so old that nobody can tell when they were planted; and the grass is so thick and soft that your feet are almost buried in it while walking. In the parks, are pretty gray deer, with timid little fawns keeping close beside their mothers, and almost afraid to be looked at. There are, also, rabbits, hares, partridges, and

Windsor Castle.

many other kinds of animals and birds, which make the parks pleasant.

4. Near the castle, is often a village of **neat white cottages**, with its church, its schoolhouse, and its shops. Around the village, are fields of golden wheat waving in the summer sunshine, and green pastures full of sheep and cows, quietly cropping the grass or dozing

in the shade. There are meadows, too, where the farmers are piling the fragrant new-mown hay on the great carts; while boys and girls follow the load with their rakes to gather up every bit that falls.

5. Haymaking and harvest are merry times in England for both young and old; but I think you would like the spring best, when the hedges are white with flowers, when the orchards are rosy, and there are so many little singing birds that you almost believe every blossom has a voice.

6. There are such green fields, neat hedges, old castles, and pretty villages, all over England; but there are many people in England who never see any of them, — many children who never see the lambs skip in the pastures, never hear the birds sing, never rake hay in the meadows, nor gather flowers from the hedges and the pastures in springtime.

7. There are mountains in England, — not very high ones, it is true, not even so high as the Appalachians; but they are very important, because they are full of iron, coal, copper, tin, and other valuable minerals. To get these things from the earth, somebody must go away out of the sunshine, out of sight of the green fields, out of hearing of the pretty singing birds; and live and work down deep within the earth, where the sun never shines, and no sound is ever heard but the voices and hammers of the miners, and the creaking of their machinery. There they stay all the time, working under the ground, sometimes not seeing the sunlight for a whole year.

8. Do you suppose you, or any child, would like to live in such a place? Yet there used to be many chil-

dren who lived there year after year, working in the mines with their fathers and brothers. There were not many things which they were strong enough to do; but they opened and shut the gates between different parts of the mine, when the loads of ore were passing, and did other things of that kind, for which they did not need to be very strong. When they went up out of the mine, they all, men and children, got into a kind of basket, and were drawn up, very much as you draw water out of a well in a bucket.

II.—THE CITIES IN ENGLAND.

Thames [*Temz*].　|　**Lon'-don** [*Lun'-dun*].　|　**Man'-ches-ter.**

1. THERE are large cities in England, where very many people live, and buy and sell goods, or work in factories and mills of different kinds. One of these, named *London*, is the largest city in the world. You might start from one side of it early in the morning, and walk all day, passing nothing but houses and shops and churches and other buildings, and yet you would hardly reach the opposite side of it before night.

2. This great city is built on both sides of the River *Thames*, not very far from the seashore. There is often much fog in the air, from the river and the sea. It is not a light, thin fog, such as you sometimes see on a summer morning above the little brooks and ponds in the country; but the smoke from the many thousand chimneys of this great city mingles with it, and makes it almost black. Sometimes it is so dark that the people are obliged to light lamps in their houses and in the

streets in the middle of the day. Even then they may lose their way in going from their shops to their homes, because they cannot see enough to know through what streets they are passing.

3. Many fine bridges cross the Thames, binding the

London and the Thames River.

parts of the city together; and, besides these, there is a passage, or *tunnel*, under the river, from one side of it to the other. There are thousands of ships all the time upon the stream. Some are coming into the city from all parts of the world, with food, clothing, and many other things for the multitudes of people who live there. Others are going out, loaded with articles to be sold in distant countries.

4. Besides the great ships and steamers, little steamboats are constantly moving up and down the river, like stages, to take passengers from one part of the long city to another; while others carry people back and forth, across the stream. Along its banks, are great warehouses for storing goods, and miles of wharves and docks, to furnish room for loading and unloading the vessels.

5. In other parts of the city, are large, beautiful parks. One, which is very fine, has the royal palace looking down upon it. There are many splendid palaces, many grand old churches, and famous public buildings, that you would like to see.

6. *Manchester* is another great city of England, though it is not nearly so large as London. You will see here a multitude of cotton factories, with great smoking chimneys. The whole city seems filled with them; and a large part of the people are in some way concerned in them. These mills make the beautiful calicoes and muslins which are used all over England, and are also packed in boxes, and sent by shiploads to all parts of the world.

7. *Liverpool* is another important city. It is near Manchester, on the seashore. Until lately, all the trade by sea with Manchester passed through its port. But now, Manchester is itself connected with the ocean by a ship canal, so that it is able to send away and receive cargoes without being obliged to depend on Liverpool. There are very many other cities in England about which you will like to learn at another time; and there are so

many railroads, that the whole country seems covered with a network of iron bands.

III.—SCOTLAND AND IRELAND.

High'-land-ers. | **Ed'-in-burgh** [-*bur-ruh*]. | **Em'-er-ald.**

1. SCOTLAND is not much like England, but is full of hills and rugged mountains. Some of them have high, steep slopes, with bare, black rocks, and, in many places, terrible precipices, which make traveling dangerous. Some of these mountains are covered with thick forests of pines and fir trees. In the winter they are loaded with snow, and look very beautiful.

2. On the lower mountains and hills, are many green pastures; and all summer you will see them covered with flocks of sheep, for most of the people in these mountain lands are shepherds. Boys and girls, and sometimes men, stay with their flocks all day, to watch them, and keep them from getting lost in the forest.

3. To help them guard the sheep, the shepherds have fine, intelligent dogs. When a sheep is lost, the shepherd's dog will be sure to find where it has gone; and, if he sees one going too far away from the flock, he will run after it, and drive it back. At night the flocks are driven into a *fold*, and the dogs alone guard them.

4. Among these mountains, there are many streams with fine waterfalls, and many beautiful, clear mountain lakes, like those in New England. In the forests, deer abound; and the *Highlanders*, as the people of the mountain country are called, are very fond of hunting them

5. Scotland is quite a cold country, and has a great deal of rainy weather. One rainy day a traveler asked a Scotchman if it rained so all the time. "No, sir," said he, "sometimes it snows." What do you think of a country in which it rains or snows most of the time?

6. Scotland contains many cities, but none are so large as the great cities in England. *Edinburgh* is the

Lake Katrine.

finest, though not the largest. It is built on hills with narrow valleys between them. Some valleys, though they have no rivers, have bridges across them, to save the trouble of going up and down. In crossing these bridges, you see houses and shops underneath, instead of water.

7. There is one hill with a fine old castle on the top'; and another that has pleasant walks winding around it to the summit, and many beautiful statues and build-

ings scattered among trees and flowers. From these hills, you can see, not only the country all about, but also the ocean. The air is clear and fresh, and not filled with fog and smoke as in London. Many of the streets are broad and pleasant; but others are so narrow, that people standing in their doorways can shake hands with their neighbors on the other side of the street.

Blarney Castle.

8. IRELAND has an abundance of rain, and is a warmer country than either England or Scotland. Its plains and hills are always fresh and green, and it is often called the *Emerald Isle*. It is the first land of Europe reached by the steamers which cross the broad ocean; and you can imagine how charming it must look to travelers who have seen nothing, during the entire voyage, but the blue sky above and the blue sea below.

The southern part is full of hills and low mountains, and among them are the most beautiful lakes and streams.

9. In many parts of the country, there are places in which the moist ground seems to be one mass of decayed vegetable matter. These are *peat bogs*. The turf, or peat, when gathered and dried, is burned instead of wood. It makes a hot fire, and is almost the only fuel of the country people; for wood is very scarce.

IV.—FRANCE.—THE COUNTRY.

chest'-nut [*ches'-*]. | **peas'-ant** [*pez'-*]. | **mu-si'-cian** [*-zi'-shan*].

1. FRANCE, on the continent of Europe, is but a short distance from Great Britain. The two countries are separated by the *English Channel*, the narrowest part of which is the *Strait of Dover*.

2. This is a pleasant land, full of broad plains, green hills, and fresh valleys; and in some parts are rugged mountains. It is much warmer than England. In the north, there is very often foggy and cloudy or rainy weather; but in the south the air is clearer, and the sky more sunny.

3. Still I think that people who travel in France do not admire this country so much as England; for the owners of the land do not take the same pains to make it beautiful. But you will see in some places what you do not see in England. In the warmer parts, there are large orchards of fig trees full of their soft, sweet fruit; groves of olive and mulberry trees; and an abundance

of peaches, pomegranates, and other excellent fruits, which do not grow in England, because it is not warm enough.

4. You will find, in other places, apple, pear, and plum trees, sometimes growing by the roadside; fields of wheat and other grain, and of beets raised for sugar; and flax, with its slender pale-green stalk, and its pretty blue flowers, like bright eyes looking up to the sunlight. In the forests which grow on the hills and mountains, are tall elms, and oaks full of glossy brown acorns, and beeches that bear the little three-cornered nuts which all children like.

5. But the best of all the trees for the country people, or *peasants*, who live on these rough lands, is the *chestnut*. You have all eaten chestnuts, and like them, I presume; but what would you think of having only roasted chestnuts, and a piece of oatmeal bread, and a cup of water, for breakfast, or dinner, or supper? The peasants use chestnuts as a part of their food. These grow much larger than the American chestnut; and sometimes, were it not for them, many persons would starve.

6. What I think would please you most, are the *vineyards*, which can be seen in all the warmer parts of France. You would not think them very beautiful; for the vines are planted by the side of wooden stakes, hardly higher than your head, above which the main stalk is never allowed to grow. The branches extend from one stake to another, and form long lines of vines, with spaces between them only wide enough to walk in.

7. But, if you go to the vineyard when the fruit is ripe, you will see, as you walk through the narrow

paths, large clusters of delicious grapes on each side, from the top to the bottom of the vines. They fill the air with their delightful fragrance, and if you put them in your mouth, you will find their taste even finer than their odor; and you may forget to notice that the vineyard looks not a little like a field of potato vines.

Vintage in France.

8. Now, early in the morning, the boys and girls, and men and women, come out from the neighboring villages, each with basket in hand, and then what a merry time they have! They laugh and sing, tell funny stories, and do all sorts of amusing things while filling their baskets, and their mouths too, with the delicious fruit.

9. Every little while, you will see a strong man carry-

ing on his back a great, deep basket, fastened to his shoulders, and reaching above the top of his head. Into this the people who are gathering the grapes, empty their smaller baskets. When it is filled, he carries it away to the road which runs through the middle, or by the side, of the vineyard, and empties his juicy load into casks ready to receive it.

10. By the side of each, is a man having in his hands a crusher, like a mallet with a long handle. As fast as the grapes are put into the casks, they are pressed, in order to break the skins, so that the juice may escape. When the casks are all full of the crushed grapes, they are driven away to the press. There the juice is pressed out, and then stored away, and left to ferment and become wine.

11. All this the merry French people greatly enjoy. Sometimes in the evening, after they have been all day gathering grapes, the owner of the vineyard employs musicians to play for them. They dance until they are tired, and then go to their homes and sleep until the morning comes to give them another such merry day. The vineyards all belong to the rich people, but the peasants are very glad to help gather the grapes.

12. There are very many people in France. For this reason there is not much land for each one of the peasants, and some of them are very poor. They do not eat white bread every day, with plenty of meat and butter, as our farmers do; but they have a kind of black bread, that is quite heavy and bitter. The most fortunate have a chicken, or a piece of pork, on Sunday; but many have meat only once a year, and that on Christmas.

13. This seems strange to you, and I suppose you

think they cannot be very happy. But they are the merriest people in the world; and the little black-eyed, black-haired, rosy-cheeked peasant boys and girls, with their bare feet, coarse dresses, and brown bread and chestnuts, are just as happy as children who have much more than they.

V.—SOME FRENCH CITIES.

bou'-le-vard [*boo'-le-var*].   mu-se'-um.   Mar-seilles' [*-sales'*].
Tui'-le-ries [*Twe'-le-riz*].   e-ly'-sian [*-lizh'-an*].   Louvre [*Loovr*].
No'-tre Dame [*No'-tr Dahm*].   Seine [*Sane*].   Med'-i-ter-ra'-ne-an.

1. FRANCE, like England, is full of fine, large cities. The largest is *Paris*, the capital, and one of the most magnificent cities in the world. Extending all round the inner part of the town, are handsome streets, called *boulevards*. They have a broad carriage way in the middle, then rows of fine trees, beneath which are sidewalks as wide as a common street, and as smooth as a floor.

2. Handsome vehicles, drawn by splendid horses, are constantly rolling along the carriage way; while the sidewalks are thronged with elegantly dressed people. But the boulevards are gayest in the evening, when the shops that border them are all brilliantly lighted; and the display of carriages and merry people is even greater than during the day.

3. In these shops, and others all over Paris, you will find all sorts of most beautiful goods. There are silks, laces, muslins, bonnets, and shawls, and handsome cloths of all kinds for ladies' and gentlemen's clothing. There

are shops full of elegant jewelry, and others where all sorts of ornaments for parlors are kept. The toy shops are a wonder, containing almost everything that any boy or girl could desire. It would take a long time to name even a small part of the toys; but think of those you admire and wish for most, and you may be sure that they can be found in the shops of Paris.

4. Here, also, are spacious gardens, in which are groves of trees, and clusters of bright flowers, with numerous monuments scattered among them, and fountains cooling the air. Pleasant walks and broad carriage ways wind among the trees and flowers; and neat benches are placed in the most beautiful spots, where people may sit with their friends, and enjoy the charming scenes. These gardens are always filled with merry people, riding, walking, or resting; and, when lighted in the evening, they are very gay places.

5. In the *Elysian Fields*, and in the *Gardens of the Tuileries*, you may always find a throng of children with their nurses. Here are kept pretty little carriages, drawn by goats, in which the children may ride about if they like; and, as you may suppose, they find it delightful to do so. There are also halls, or galleries, filled with rare and beautiful paintings and statues; and museums of curious things that have been collected from all parts of the world. There is one place, called the *Garden of Plants*, in which is a collection of living plants and animals, from all countries.

6. Paris is built on both sides of the River *Seine*, and, like London, has many bridges, some of which are very handsome. It is adorned with arches and columns, erected by the different kings and emperors who have

ruled over France, in honor of their brave and wise men, or of the victories which their armies have gained. There are, also, many famous churches and palaces. You will often hear of the *Notre Dame*, one of the finest churches, of the *Tuileries*, which was once the emperor's palace, and of the *Louvre*, with its beautiful paintings.

Tuileries.

7. Another of the cities of France is celebrated far and wide, on account of the elegant silk goods which are made there. This is *Lyons*. Almost half the people of the city are workers in silk. These silk makers do not work constantly in great factories full of machinery, as do the people who make cotton goods in Manchester. They have little machines in their own houses; and, hiring two or three other people to help

them, they weave the beautiful pieces of silk, ribbon, or velvet, when ordered by the silk merchants.

8. Sometimes they have nothing to do for a long while, and suffer much, because this is their only way of getting money. They all live in one part of the city, on a hill between the two rivers on the banks of which Lyons is built. The largest of these is the *Rhone*, of which you will learn more another time.

9. The hills that slope up from the river banks are covered with tall, beautiful buildings shaded with fine trees, and are ornamented with many noble monuments. This makes the city look very pleasant; but, if you go about, you will not like it so well. The streets are narrow and disagreeable; and by the side of magnificent structures, you will often find ruinous old houses, and dust and dirt so thick that you can hardly bear to walk about.

10. The streets that lead up the hillsides are very crooked, and sometimes so steep that it has been necessary to make stairways in some places. But, after you are upon the top of the highest hill, you will feel well repaid for the hard walk you have had. From this hilltop you can see the whole city, with the two rivers gliding like silver bands among its beautiful buildings; the green valley of the Rhone, with the great plain at the west of it; and even, far away to the east, the high *Alps*, looking like masses of purple clouds.

11. *Marseilles* is another fine city. It is on the coast of the *Mediterranean* Sea, — an arm of the Atlantic which separates Europe from Africa. This is a much warmer place than Paris or Lyons, and has much less rain. It is in that part of France which has the bright,

sunny sky, where the grapes grow so rich and sweet. The city is built around a little bay, and has a fine harbor, where you may see ships from all parts of the world, and hear many different languages spoken.

12. One part is called the *Old City*. In this the streets are narrow, and the houses are high and old and dark. The other part, called the *New City*, has straight, broad streets, with fine houses and numerous shops, like those of Paris. One street has many beautiful fountains, supplied with water, brought in a canal from the hills many miles away.

13. The country around Marseilles is not all beautiful like that around Lyons. In some places it is very dry, and you can hardly see a green leaf or a blade of grass. The houses have nothing to make it pleasant about them but the sea view. This is so charming, with the blue and quiet waters dotted with green islands, and the clear, sunny sky overhead, that it makes one almost forget how dreary it is on the land. But other parts have no need of a view of the sea to make them pleasing; for there are green valleys filled with vineyards, and groves of olive, orange, and mulberry trees.

14. These are not all of the fine cities in France. There are others in the interior as remarkable for cotton mills, linen factories, and iron works as Lyons for its silk looms; and still others on the coast, which are famous as markets for wine, brandy, and fruits, or for the elegant manufactures of the country. But, after all, France is not nearly so crowded as Great Britain; for, though more than twice as large, it has not so many great cities; and Paris itself is but little more than half the size of London.

VI. — THE NETHERLANDS, BELGIUM, AND THE NORTHERN COUNTRIES.

| Hol'-land. | Am'-ster-dam. | Den'-mark. |
| Bel'-gi-um. | Swe'-den. | Nor-we'-gi-an. |

1. THE Netherlands (or Holland), a small but very interesting country, lies in the low plains about the mouth of the Rhine. The ground is so low and flat

Amsterdam.

that it is hard work to keep the sea from overflowing, and covering it entirely. There are many lakes and marshes along the shore. The people build, around these, banks of earth, called *dikes*, to keep out the sea, then pump the water from them until they are dry, and so change them into rich meadows.

2. **Canals** run all through the country, to drain away the water; and in summer you will see the people moving about in little boats, instead of going in carriages, by roads, as in other countries. In winter the canals all freeze over, and then are covered with skaters. The farmers' wives skate to market, the men to business, and the children to school.

3. The Netherlanders are called Dutch, and it was from this country that the people came who first settled New York. They are very industrious, and nowhere in the world will you find better farmers than they. The rich meadows are full of fine sleek cows, from the milk of which excellent butter and cheese are made. The Dutch are great fishermen, too. They catch herring in the sea between England and the Netherlands, but go to distant parts of the ocean for the cod and the whale.

Dutch Windmill.

4. *Amsterdam* is a city of the Netherlands. It is full of canals instead of streets; and the ships which bring goods to the merchants can sail to the doors of the shops, to be unloaded.

5. BELGIUM lies between the Netherlands and France, on the seashore opposite England. It is much like the Netherlands, but not so flat, nor so damp. It is more

densely peopled than any other country in Europe. The land is divided into little farms not larger than a common field in one of the farms of our country. But the soil is so fertile, and the farmer is so very industrious, that, small as his field seems to us, he is able to get a living from it.

6. He sows wheat in one corner, and rye in another, some clover for the cows in one part, and some flax, to make linen for clothing, in still another. The cows are kept in a stable, and the children must gather weeds and grass to feed them. Besides, there is a pig, and some hens, and sometimes a goat, to be taken care of; and the house to be kept clean, and the flax to be spun. Thus, you see, there is enough for all to do.

7. DENMARK, SWEDEN, and NORWAY are still farther north. Denmark and southern Sweden are low lands, but much colder than the Netherlands. Norway is a high, rugged, mountainous country, and is very cold. The tops of the mountains are covered with snow, from which great masses of ice creep down to the valleys, sometimes reaching even to the seashore. Here they are often broken; and the part falling into the sea forms an iceberg, which goes floating away toward the warmer parts of the ocean until it melts.

8. On the lower slopes of the mountains, are tall, dense forests of pines and fir trees. Rich ores of iron, also, abound. The coasts are thronged with wild ducks and geese and other water fowl, and the sea is filled with excellent fish. The hardy farm products also thrive in all the warmer portions.

9. Many of the Norwegians work in the forests, cutting down the tall, straight trees, which they send

away to Denmark, Germany, and even to England and France, to be used for masts of vessels. Great numbers work in the mines, or catch fish along the coast; and many, also, are shepherds.

10. In summer the cattle and sheep are driven away to the mountain pastures, where they are taken care of by children and by the old people, while the strong men

Laplanders.

are busy in the forests, the mines, or the fisheries. The Laplanders, in the northern part of Sweden and Norway, obtain almost their whole living from the reindeer. They feed upon its milk and flesh, make their clothing and tents of its skin, and train it to draw their sledges from place to place in winter. The rocky coast is often broken by narrow clefts, or *fiords*.

VII.—SPAIN.

Ma-drid'. | Pyr'-e-nees. | Pa'-los [Pah'-].
me-ri'-no [-ree'-]. | Por'-tu-gal. | Span'-iard.

1. SPAIN is a large country lying on the coast southwest of France. Between them is a high mountain range. Its steep slopes are covered with forests, and are broken by narrow valleys, full of clear, rapid streams, with hundreds of foaming waterfalls. High up above the forests, whose glossy green leaves are never blackened by frosts, are handsome flowering shrubs and mosses. Still higher are the bare mountain peaks, covered nearly all the year with snow and ice.

2. This mountain range is the *Pyrenees*. The passes that lead over it are difficult and dangerous everywhere, except at the extremities of the range. The forests are the home of many mountain goats, and other fleet, sure-footed animals, which leap from rock to rock with the greatest agility.

3. Crossing the Pyrenees, and going southward, we find ourselves at length on a high table-land, — the roof of Spain, as it might be called. It is dry, sterile, and so dusty, that even the few cultivated fields seem hardly less dreary than they would be without a green leaf upon them. The small, poor villages are so covered with the dust blown upon them by the terrible winds, that they become as gray as the ground, and at a short distance can hardly be distinguished from it.

4. Here and there the high, dreary table-land is cut by a deep valley, through which flows a river; and

in these valleys, sheltered from the sweeping winds, are beautiful orchards and gardens. But elsewhere little grows except poor, coarse grasses. In spring and autumn these furnish pasture for thousands of fine-wooled *merino* sheep; but in the long dry summer the whole surface is parched and dead. Now the merinos are driven northward to fresh pastures near the mountains. In winter they go down into the sheltered valleys to escape the storms and the cold, which are very severe.

5. From this high table-land in the center of Spain, long mountain ranges, having broad, beautiful valleys between them, extend away to the sea at the east, south, and west. These mountains are rugged and broken. Many are covered with forests, which are the homes of multitudes of wolves; while the glens and caves are frequently the shelter of robbers. Thus traveling in the mountainous regions is not only unpleasant, but often dangerous.

6. In the forests, are many valuable trees. Among them is a kind of oak, the bark of which is the *cork*, so useful in many ways. Another oak bears a small, sweet acorn, which is much relished by the people. It is eaten either uncooked, or boiled or roasted, as the French peasants eat chestnuts. Were we visiting in the parts of the country where it grows, it would be offered to us as a great delicacy.

7. The highest of the mountain ranges in Spain, like the highest in California, is called the *Sierra Nevada*, because its summit is covered with snow, even in midsummer. In the warm, rich valleys at its foot are orange, olive, and mulberry groves, and gardens of

pineapples, bananas, and beautiful flowers. No frost ever withers them; and no winter's cold robs them of their leaves, their flowers, or their fruits.

8. The *olive*, though a very useful tree, is not at all a handsome one. Its long narrow leaves are thick and stiff, and are of a dull grayish color, as though covered with dust. The branches are rough and crooked; and the trunk looks as though a strong hand had seized it by the top, and twisted it, as we twist a cord. In spring it is covered with clusters of pretty white flowers, and in autumn with the small, dark-green, plum-shaped fruit from which the olive oil, often called sweet oil, is pressed. The fruit is also preserved, and sent to other countries to be used as a relish at meals.

Olive Tree and Fruit.

9. Do you wish to know the use of the mulberry trees? Their leaves furnish the food of the silkworm. Very many of these worms are raised in Spain. When they have lived a certain length of time, and are grown to their full size, they spin a fine thread, which they wind round their bodies until they are completely wrapped up in it. Thus they form a ball somewhat like that made by the caterpillar, from which a butterfly comes in the spring. This ball of thread which the

silkworm spins is called a *cocoon*. Large quantities of cocoons are sent to Lyons, to be unwound and woven into elegant silks.

10. There are not such great and busy cities in Spain as in England and France. The largest is *Madrid*, the capital of the country. It is on the high table-land, in the interior, far from the sea. No ships can come near it; and it is without any large river upon which boats can go to the sea, or to other parts of the country.

Mulberry and Silkworm.

11. Madrid is very cold in winter, and very hot in summer, and so is not an agreeable place in which to live. Still the fountains playing in all parts of the city in the summer make it look very pleasant, and cool the air nicely. The water, like that of the fountains in Marseilles, comes from the country many miles away, and is pure and cool.

12. The people of Madrid do little work. In the morning the men walk idly to and fro, with a long cloak over their shoulders, and a broad crimson sash, in which a large knife is always hidden, tied about the waist. The women wear long, rich dresses, with a shawl around them, and an elegant lace scarf thrown over their heads instead of a bonnet.

13. After dinner every one, even the workman, sleeps for several hours. In the evening people go to walk on the *Prado*, a beautiful, broad walk two miles in length, which runs through the city. Rows of elm trees, with seats arranged beneath them, shade it; and here and there are fountains playing, around which are persons with little cups, waiting to sell water to those who are thirsty.

14. Along the seashore are many cities, from which are shipped choice fruits, both fresh and dried, wines, and olive oil. On the southern coast is a little old town, called *Palos*, now all going to ruin. From this town, about four hundred years ago, three small ships, furnished by the king and queen of Spain, sailed away under the command of Christopher Columbus. They went in search of lands which Columbus believed might be found beyond the Atlantic Ocean. He was sure that the earth was round, and that he could go to the Indies by sailing westward.

Fleet of Columbus.

15. When they came back, after some months, they

brought tidings of a new land and a new people on the other side of the ocean; for they had reached some islands of the West Indies. Columbus made other voyages, and found South America; and soon after, North America was reached by another expedition. Thus the Spaniards discovered the New World. It was they who made the first settlements there, and who conquered and destroyed the rich old cities in **Mexico** and the valleys of the Andes.

16. On the west side of Spain, between a part of its territory and the Atlantic, is a narrow strip of country so much like Spain, that the traveler would hardly see any difference between them. This is PORTUGAL. Like its greater neighbor, Portugal is famed for its warm, fruitful valleys and the fine wines from its vineyards.

VIII.—ITALY.

| Ven'-ice [-iss]. | Ve-su'-vi-us. | Her-cu-la'-ne-um. |
| gon'-do-la. | Na'-ples [-plz]. | Pom-pe'-ii [-pa'-ye]. |

1. ITALY is in the southern part of Europe. It is nearly surrounded by the Mediterranean Sea, and is one of the hottest countries on the continent. The sky is almost always blue and clear; and the country, with its mountains and green valleys, its vineyards and meadows, is always pleasant. People from all over the world go to Italy to enjoy the sunny sky and the charming country, and to see the fine pictures and statues, and the remains of magnificent buildings, made by the old Romans who lived there hundreds of years ago.

ITALY. 141

2. The sun is so very bright, that most things grow better by being somewhat shaded. For this reason you will see the fields planted with rows of trees, — mulberries and olives, elms, poplars, and a kind of pine which thrives only in warm countries. Around the

A Lake in Italy.

foot of these the grapevines are planted. They climb the tree, and cover its branches; and shoots of the vine go from one tree to another, hanging between them in graceful festoons. Between the rows of trees, wheat and corn are planted, and fine crops are produced. You see, therefore, that a vineyard in Italy is a very different thing from one in France. The tall grain, the branches of the trees, and the slender twigs of the grapevine, waving in the wind under the blue sunny sky, make, as you may suppose, a very pretty picture.

3. Sometimes, near a city, the road for miles is bordered on each side by rows of grapevines. These, climbing upon trees or upon a sort of framework, meet over the road, making a pleasant shaded way for the traveler. The rich ripe grapes delight him with their fragrance, and he is allowed to gather all he wants to eat as he goes along; but he must not gather them to take away, for that would be robbing other travelers who may come after him. How would you like to travel in this country?

4. Italy contains very many old cities. They were once full of wealthy people, with splendid palaces, churches, and buildings of all kinds; but the noble palaces have gone to ruin, and only the precious marble of which they were built remains to tell us how grand they once were.

5. *Rome* is the most remarkable of these cities. It was built more than two thousand years ago by a brave and skillful people, who did everything to make it grand and beautiful. When our Savior came on the earth, the emperor of Rome ruled over nearly all of the world then known to the Romans.

6. There is in Rome one of the finest churches in the world, named *St. Peter's;* also a very fine old palace, in which lives the *pope*, the head of the Roman Catholic Church. In both of these buildings you find valuable paintings and sculptures made by men who have been dead hundreds of years. Although these have

been studied by the great artists from all countries, yet none have ever produced works of higher merit.

7. There are many grand palaces in Rome which are famous for their fine galleries of paintings and sculptures, or for their beautiful gardens. Some are surrounded by orange trees, covered with snowy fragrant

Venice.

flowers or delicious golden fruit gleaming among the glossy leaves.

8. If you stand on the shore in the northeastern part of Italy, and look away over the water, you will see, a long way off, palaces and towers which seem to rise from the midst of the waves, for you see no land around them. This is *Venice*, another famous old Italian city. It was built on a great number of small flat islands; and

its churches and palaces were adorned with marbles of the finest colors, or with white marble handsomely sculptured. These, with the sunny sky above them, and the calm blue waters below, made it one of the most beautiful cities in the world.

9. Venice is still very handsome, though many of its finest buildings are almost in ruins. Graceful little boats, called *gondolas*, glide about from place to place in the quiet waters between the islands. The merry songs of the gondoliers sound much more pleasant than the rattling of carriages and heavy carts over the rough pavements, which in other cities almost deafens us.

10. There are in Italy many cities besides these interesting old ones, though there are none so large or so important as those of England and France. *Naples* is in the south of Italy, where there is hardly a touch of winter. It is built on the seashore, with a broad blue bay in front, and rough hills and fresh green valleys all around it. The valleys and hills are covered with orange groves and vineyards.

11. At a little distance, is the famous volcano of *Vesuvius*, from which clouds of vapor are always rising. Its lower slopes are cultivated like the surrounding country; though the people know that at any time the volcano may send out a stream of lava to burn, or a shower of cinders to bury, them all.

12. At times, when the orange groves and vineyards are bathed in the beautiful sunlight, the cattle quietly feeding in the pastures, and the people peacefully working or resting in their pleasant homes, a sudden noise like thunder is heard in the earth, and the mountain begins to tremble. The animals run about in terror,

and the people know that they must hasten to escape the danger that is coming. They go away to Naples or to some other place, far enough from the mountain to be safe. On coming back, they sometimes find their vineyards and villages all destroyed; but they are not afraid to settle themselves again upon the slopes, for they know that the volcano is not likely to do any more harm for years.

13. Two cities, that stood near Naples, were once buried under substances thrown out from Vesuvius. Their names were *Herculaneum* and *Pompeii*. For nearly eighteen hundred years no one knew the place where they had been; but now they have been found, and parts of them are uncovered. People can enter the houses, and see how they were arranged, and how people lived in those old times. Many curious and beautiful things, made before our Savior came into the world, are found in these buried cities.

IX. — SWITZERLAND.

Swit'-zer-land. | av'-a-lanche. | cham'-ois [*sham'-my*].
Ge-ne'-va. | gla'-cier [*glā'-sher*]. | al'-pine [-*pin*].

1. SWITZERLAND is a small but famous country east of France. The first thing one thinks of in hearing this name is the *Alps*, a high, rugged mountain range. Its lower slopes are covered with vineyards, orchards, wheat fields, and meadows, with pleasant villages in every valley. Higher up are green forests of oak and walnut, then tall, dark pines and firs.

146   *GEOGRAPHICAL READER.*

2. Above these, are clusters of low shrubs covered with bright flowers, and green pastures, with hundreds of sleek cows feeding upon them. Little cottages are scattered all about, for the men who take care of the cows. Still higher are the tall sharp peaks, cov-

View in the Alps.

ered with ice and snow, and glistening like silver in the sunshine. These are the highest mountains in Europe, and among the grandest in the world. They fill all the southern half of Switzerland, and separate it from Italy.

3. Thousands of streams flow through the pleasant

green valleys, leaping over precipices, and making fine waterfalls. Some of these are so high, that the water, in falling, changes into fine spray; and the fall looks like a shower of white dust coming from the sky. Sometimes the streams go leaping and dancing into little basinlike hollows, or deep gorges among the mountains. These make beautiful lakes, that smile in the sunshine, reflecting the snowy peaks above them or the green forests around.

4. High up in the mountains, beyond the forests and green pastures, the valleys are no longer gay with streams that dance and sparkle and sing; but in their stead are *rivers of ice*, creeping along so slowly, so very slowly, that they seem not to move at all. It is only after watching them a long time, and trying them in many ways, that people have found out that they do move. They are called *glaciers*.

5. In the cold winter, the sides of the valleys containing glaciers look very dreary, all buried in deep snow; but, when the spring comes, the snow melts away, and there is left only the great ice river in the valley. The mountain slopes on both sides of it are covered with fresh green grass and pretty mountain flowers. How strange that must seem! Sometimes flowers grow and blossom, even on the top of the ice, in the little heaps of earth that have gathered there by falling from the rocks above.

6. These ice rivers go over precipices too, and make cataracts of ice all broken and split into every possible shape. Some of them are very grand. In the lower valleys, where the summer is quite warm, the end of the glacier melts away as fast as it descends. Thus it

advances no farther, but the melting ice forms a fine stream of water. The Rhone, which flows through Lyons, in France, springs, in this way, from one of the glaciers of the Alps.

7. Up among the snowy peaks, from which the glaciers descend, terrible *avalanches* are sometimes formed. During or after a winter storm, a mass of snow becomes loosened from the rock on which it fell, and begins to

Lake Geneva.

roll down the mountain. As it moves onward, the snow on which it rolls clings to it, making it larger and heavier every moment, until it becomes an immense body. Now it rushes along as swiftly as the wind, dashing down the forest trees in its path, and never stopping until it has reached the valley at the foot of the slope, where it sometimes buries whole villages.

8. The whole of Switzerland is only a knot of moun-

tains and green valleys, sparkling with streams and clear mountain lakes. Every little valley has its villages, and all the larger ones have pleasant cities, many of which are beside the beautiful lakes. You see, therefore, that, though a small country, it contains many inhabitants. They are a strong, brave people, who love their mountains and valleys so much, that they can never bear to leave them, and are ready to fight and die for their homes.

9. The peasants, who have their small farms on the mountains, keep cows and goats; and many of them spend the whole summer making cheese. As soon as the snow is gone, the men go with their herds up to the high mountain pastures. There they stay until the snow comes again in the autumn, living in little cottages in the pastures, taking care of their cows, and having scarcely anything but milk and cheese to eat. In autumn they come down again, bringing with them their cheeses, which they sell in the cities.

10. It is a very merry time when the cows go to the pastures in the spring. The whole village to which the herdsmen belong has a holiday; and their friends go with them part of the way, shouting, singing, and making themselves merry in every way.

11. In many villages, all the winter, the people are carving from wood curious vases, knives, boxes, spoons, figures of cheese makers, of hunters with their chamois, and many other things. These are sold as curiosities to travelers who visit the mountains.

12. Some of the valleys, though quite high and cold, are yet full of pleasant villages and cities, where almost everybody is making watches. *Geneva* is the great mar-

ket of the watchmakers. It is a very beautiful town beside *Lake Geneva*, one of the largest lakes of the country.

X.—GERMANY.

Dan'-ube. | Rhine [*Ri*ne]. | Mu'-nich [-*nik*].
Ger'-ma-ny. | Ber'-lin. | Prus'-sia [*Prush'*-].

1. THERE is a broad mountain land extending northward from the Alps, the mountains becoming constantly lower and lower. Two great rivers flow through it,— the *Danube*, going east; and the *Rhine*, going north. They are the longest rivers in all the western part of Europe.

2. This mountain country is divided into many little states,—almost as many as there are separate ranges and different valleys and basins. In all these the German language is spoken; and they are united into one great empire called *Germany*. Thus Germany is not the name of a single state, like France or England, but of many united.

3. The southern part is much like Switzerland, with its mountains covered with dark forests and green pastures; its woodcutters, chamois hunters, and milkmen; and its mountain villages, wood carvers, and toy makers. It is full of deep gorges, bordered by high and sometimes very steep walls of rock, and is the most interesting part of Germany.

4. Here and there, on the top of the highest rocks, is a gray old castle, where, years ago, bold men lived. They were always having quarrels with each other, and

put their strong castles in these places to keep out of reach of their enemies. Sometimes, while the lords of these strongholds, and their retainers, were all gone to fight one enemy, another would come to beat down the castle. Then the ladies who were left at home were obliged, with their servants, to defend it alone. There were brave ladies in those days; and sometimes they

A Castle on the Rhine.

drove the enemy away as well as the lords of the castle could have done it themselves.

5. Those things are all past now. Many of the castles are without inhabitants; and bats and owls, rats and mice, live where brave knights and fair ladies once had their home. Everybody likes to see those old castles, and think of the old times, so different from the present, and of the daring people of those days.

6. Through this rough country the Rhine flows in a broad, beautiful valley, which, like all the warm valleys of Germany, is covered with orchards and vineyards. At length the valley narrows to mountain gorges, through which the river finds its way, among crags and peaks crowned with ancient castles. Then it moves slowly onward, across low, flat plains, to the sea.

7. The part of Germany beyond the mountains is very level, and is covered with grainfields and pastures. You may see also large fields of flax, which the German women know how to spin into the finest threads for making the rich laces that all ladies so much admire. The plains extend northward to the shores of the Baltic Sea, an arm of the Atlantic Ocean.

8. In the Baltic plains, is the larger part of the kingdom of *Prussia*, the most powerful of the German countries. In the sands along the coast, is found a beautiful substance called *amber*, which you may have seen; for it is used for beads and many other ornaments. After a storm in which the waves have rolled high, and have beaten and washed away the sands of the beach, it sometimes is found in considerable quantities.

9. In the western part of Prussia, in the midst of the plains, is the great city of *Berlin*, the capital of the German Empire. This city has one of the finest streets in Europe. At one end of it is the king's palace; at the other is a splendid gate, leading through the walls into the country.

10. Berlin contains a celebrated *university*, in which young men are taught any branch of learning they desire to study. Many of the greatest scholars of Germany have studied or taught there for many years.

The university, and the learned men it has brought to Berlin, have made the city renowned all over the world. There are many other noted universities in Germany.

11. Germany has many large cities besides Berlin. some of them very old, and full of strange buildings and fine churches that were built hundreds of years ago. They have very strong, dark walls, tall towers, and multitudes of slender pinnacles; and are adorned with figures of men and animals, leaves and flowers, and many other ornaments, carved from the solid stone.

12. Some of the churches, though begun so long ago, have never been entirely finished. *Strassburg Cathedral* is one of the oldest of these. Strassburg is at the west of the Rhine, in a tract of country conquered by France from the Germans. This tract contains the two provinces Alsace and Lorraine, which were regained by Germany in the war of 1870.

Strassburg Cathedral.

13. *Munich* is one of the finest of German cities. It is famous for its valuable collections of paintings and sculptures.

XI. — AUSTRIA-HUNGARY, TURKEY, AND GREECE.

Aus'-tri-a-Hun'-ga-ry. Vi-en'-na. Con-stan-ti-no'-ple.
Tur'-key. mosque [*mosk*]. Rou-ma'-ni-a.

1. THERE is in the central part of Europe, east of Germany, a large empire called AUSTRIA-HUNGARY. The western portion includes a part of the Alps, and is much like Switzerland and southern Germany. Through this the Danube flows, winding along beautiful valleys, or rushing down deep and narrow gorges in waterfalls and rapids.

2. East of the mountains, is a fine country of low hills and rich plains, in which are forests, grainfields, and vineyards. Everywhere are villages and cities, some of which have stood for hundreds of years; and here and there, on rugged hills, are strong old castles, like those in Germany. The largest of the cities is *Vienna;* which is situated beside the Danube, near the point where it leaves the mountains. It is the capital of the empire; and contains the palaces in which the emperor and his family live, and many other splendid buildings.

3. Beyond this varied country, a broad plain stretches eastward, without hills, without trees, without roads, without houses. Along the streams are immense marshes, which it is almost impossible to cross. Elsewhere the plain is sandy, covered only by grass or other low plants. In some places, even these do not grow; but the bare, loose sand is driven by the winds into ridges like snowdrifts.

4. East and north of these great plains, is another mountainous region. It is covered with forests, and is full of rich deposits of gold and silver, copper and lead, rock salt, and many other valuable minerals. These mountain lands and the plains of the Danube are both in *Hungary*, the largest division of Austria-Hungary. It contains some of the finest and richest portions of central Europe.

5. South of Austria-Hungary is a wide region of small plains, mountain ranges, and valleys. The Black Sea is at the east of it, the Mediterranean at the south, and the Adriatic at the west. For several hundred years this was all one country, called TURKEY IN EUROPE; for the Turks, who came from Asia, conquered the native peoples.

6. Now the southern portion forms the kingdom of Greece, and the northern portion *Roumania*, and the parts next south of the Danube are also separate and independent; so that only a small strip through the middle of their former possessions is at present controlled by the Turks.

7. If you were to travel in Turkey, you would find many things to surprise you, — not in the country itself, for it is much like the other warm countries in Europe, but in the appearance and manners of its people. The men wear long, loose robes falling down to the feet. Around the waist is a broad belt, or sash, in which a sword is usually carried; and on the head is a large turban, instead of a hat.

8. The Turks have no chairs or sofas in their houses, but sit on large, soft cushions, or on rugs spread upon the floor. The Turkish ladies are not

taught even to read and are never allowed to go into the street, unless veiled so that only their eyes can be seen. Then even their own husbands or fathers could not recognize them. There, it would be thought as strange for a lady to go into the street without a veil, as, in this country, without shoes.

9. The Turks have a different religion from that of the other nations of Europe. They are followers of

Constantinople.

a man named Mohammed, who was born in Arabia, about 570 A.D. He claimed to be the only true prophet of God and became a religious teacher. His followers are called Mohammedans.

10. On the borders of Turkey the waters of the Black Sea go southwestward to the Mediterranean, making a short but most famous passage between Europe and Asia. The old Greeks had many strange legends con-

nected with this stream. Besides, the hostile armies that in old times used to pass from one continent to the other, were accustomed to cross here. It was over this stream that the ancient Persian king, Xerxes, made the bridge of boats for his soldiers to cross on when he attempted to conquer Greece.

11. Near the Black Sea, on a beautiful expansion of this outlet called the *Golden Horn*, is the great city of *Constantinople*. The sunny blue sky above, the ships with their snowy sails floating quietly on the peaceful waters, and the great city on the shore with its gilded domes and slender *minarets*, present a very delightful view.

12. The city itself looks fine as you see it from a distance; but, on entering it, you find the streets narrow, dirty, and disagreeable, and the buildings generally poor and low, though some of the churches, or *mosques*, are very elegant.

13. GREECE was the first part of Turkey in Europe to become free. It is nearly surrounded by the great Mediterranean Sea, and the Greeks are very fond of sea life. They build many ships, and are excellent sailors.

14. When the rest of Europe was peopled only by shepherds, or by tribes of half-wild men, Greece was the home of scholars and artists, — men who studied to become wise, and who produced works of art exhibiting such taste and skill, that they have ever since called forth the wonder and admiration of the most cultivated people of all nations. The country is full of the ruins of cities which in ancient times were among the most beautiful in the world. *Athens* was one of the most famous cities of the olden time.

XII.—RUSSIA.

Rus'-sia [*Rush'-*]. | Cas'-pi-an. | St. Pe'-ters-burg.

1. WE have noticed very many countries in Europe; but all these together form only about one half of the continent. The other half is one great country named RUSSIA. On the southern border is the *Black Sea*, and on the southeast another immense body of water named the *Caspian Sea*.

2. If we were to travel across Russia from north to south, we should find first a frozen country, with plants, animals, and people much like those in the coldest part of North America. South of this cold, dreary region is an immense forest, inhabited by bears, wolves, deer, and innumerable other animals, from many of which fine furs are obtained. In all this vast region not a single city, not a village, and hardly a farm, can be seen. Farther south, in the middle part of Russia, are smaller forests here and there, with cultivated lands, villages, and rich cities, as in other countries.

3. Railroads are not common all over Russia, as in the United States and England and France. For this reason, traveling by land is not so easy everywhere. In winter the travelers wrap themselves in warm fur cloaks and robes, and, with fine horses and large sleighs, glide swiftly and pleasantly over the sparkling snow. But the forests are dangerous on account of the wolves, great troops of them sometimes following the sleigh for miles.

4. In the western part of Russia, near the sea, with the great forest country at the east of it, is *St. Petersburg*,

the capital. Here it is hot in summer; but the summers are short, and the winters are long and very cold. The ground is covered with deep snow; the river beside the city is frozen; and the adjacent sea is filled with ice. The people, wrapped in furs so that you can hardly see their faces, amuse themselves in sleighing, and in sliding

The Winter Palace, St. Petersburg.

down hill. As the land about the city is flat, "ice hills" are built on purpose for this sport.

5. There is hardly another city in Europe so full of palaces and other fine buildings as St. Petersburg. The emperor's residence, called the "Winter Palace," is one of the largest and grandest in the world. Near it is a fine statue of Peter the Great on horseback.

AFRICA.

I.—SAHARA AND THE BARBARY STATES.

Sa-ha'-ra [-hah'-].　　o'-a-sis.　　Ar'-abs.
car'-a-van.　　At'-las.　　Bar'-ba-ry.

1. IN the northern part of Africa, is an immense dry, barren plain, almost as large as our whole country. As far as the eye can reach, there is only a bare, sandy surface, with occasional hills and mountains of naked rock. Hardly ever a drop of rain falls, or a cloud is seen in the sky, and never a cool breeze fans your cheek; but all the year round it is the same dry, desolate land. Such a dry, barren country is called a *desert*.

2. This is the Great Desert, or *Sahara*. Here and there, as you travel over it, you may find a little spring bubbling up from the earth, and sending a small stream of water for a short distance, until it is lost in the sand. In other places, wells have been dug from which the ground can be watered. Around the springs and wells, the earth is no longer naked, and scorching to the feet, but is covered with a rich, cool carpet of fresh grass, and shaded by groves of date trees. Such a fertile spot, like a green island in the sea of sand, is called an *oasis*. There are many oases in some parts of the desert.

3. On the larger oases are wandering *Arabs*, with flocks of sheep and goats, and many camels and horses. When the flocks have eaten all the grass upon one oasis, the Arabs go with them to another, and then another; and thus they wander from place to place all the year round. Because they must thus keep moving about all

Scene on the Sahara.

the time, these Arabs do not build houses, but live in tents, which can be taken up, and carried with them wherever they go. They are called *nomads*, or wandering people.

4. Arab merchants, in great companies called *caravans*, constantly travel across the desert, conveying goods from the countries on one side to those on the

other. These are packed in large bundles, and fastened upon the backs of camels. The food and water for the whole company are also carried by camels.

5. The desert chiefs, who take care of and guide the caravan, are mounted on beautiful, swift horses. Their saddles and bridles are trimmed with crimson velvet, and gold and silver fringes, and buttons. They wear long silk robes of bright colors, and rich turbans; and with swords by their sides, or spears in their hands, they present a very striking appearance.

6. The caravans travel during the day, and at night encamp, if possible, on some oasis; but they sometimes go on for days without finding any. Then it occasionally happens that the water brought with them gives out, and they suffer greatly. The camels can go several days without water, but the horses and men cannot; and, if they do not soon reach a spring or well, they die of thirst.

7. Besides, fierce winds often sweep over the desert, filling the air with thick clouds of sand. Some of these sand storms are so dreadful as nearly to destroy the caravans. You would think no one would wish to go into such dangers; but the Arabs love the wild life of the desert.

8. The Sahara, though so great, is not the whole of Africa, nor even half of it. There are fertile lands both north and south of it. Near the north coast of Africa, opposite Italy and Spain, is a mountain land, with fine valleys, streams, and lakes. The mountains, called the *Atlas*, are covered with forests. In the valleys are villages and cities surrounded by wheat fields and orange groves, vineyards and mulberry trees.

9. Along the coast also are cities, with ships in their harbors from many countries. This part of Africa is called *Barbary*, or the *country of the Berbers*.

II.—EGYPT AND THE NEGRO LAND.

E'-gypt [-jipt]. | **E-gyp'-tian**. | **Su-dan'** [*Soo-dahn'*].

1. EAST of the Barbary States, in the corner of Africa, is EGYPT, of which no doubt you have all heard. It is the country to which Joseph was taken when his brothers

A Boat on the River Nile.

sold him. Through it flows a great river named the *Nile*, which is one of the longest in the world. It was in the grass and rushes beside this river that Moses was hidden by his mother, in a little cradle made so that it could float on the water.

2. Egypt is a strange country, — only a narrow strip of fertile land along the river, with a desert on each side of it. It hardly ever has rain; yet it is a very fruitful country, and has always been famous for the wheat, rice, and other things that grow there. We read in the Bible, that once, when there was a famine for seven years, Jacob sent his sons to Egypt to buy corn. How do you suppose this can be, when there is no rain?

3. Every spring it rains hard in a country far south of Egypt, near the source of the Nile. This causes the river to rise, even in Egypt, and overflow its banks; and all the land around it is covered with water for several months. If you should visit Egypt at this time, you would see only what appears to be a great lake, with a boundless desert on each side, and with islands here and there, each having a village or city upon it.

4. In October the flood goes down, and leaves the ground wet, and covered with a thin coat of rich soil that has settled from the water. Just as soon as they can see the earth again, the Egyptian farmers, who do not need to plow the fields, sow the seed upon this damp new soil; and, as the country is very warm, it sprouts, and grows quickly. Where the lake was, may now be seen a broad green plain, with the river slowly gliding through it, and the villages and cities scattered here and there on little hills or mounds.

5. Frequent canals, leading from the river across the plain, are filled by the overflow with water from the

Nile; and, when the fields begin to get dry, they are watered from these, until the plants are grown and ready to be gathered. Thus, you see, it is the water of the Nile that keeps Egypt from being a desert.

6. South of the Sahara is the part of Africa in which the negroes live. There are lakes, almost as large as the largest of our country, with great rivers flowing

Negro Houses in South Africa.

from them, through fertile regions, to the sea. These are the sources of the Nile. On the borders of some are wide marshes, covered with reeds and cane, in which multitudes of animals hide to sleep, or to watch for their prey.

7. In other places, the whole broad country, for hundreds of miles, is one great forest. The trees are always green,— growing, blooming, and bearing their fruits at

all times in the year. Here, too, are the great elephant, the terrible lion, the tall giraffe, besides a multitude of other animals; for in Africa are gathered, in greater numbers than in any other continent, the largest, strongest, and most beautiful animals in the world.

8. The part next south of the Sahara is called *Sudan*. It is a middle region, between the barren lands of the desert, and the vast forests of Central Africa; and the country consists of rich, treeless plains alternating with woodlands. Here are found the best of the negro tribes.

9. The negroes of Sudan raise grain, cotton, and other things. They know how to make cloth from the cotton, and to make, from iron and copper, such tools as they need. They live together in towns and villages, which are mere collections of huts, looking entirely unlike anything we ever saw.

10. In the extreme south the coast lands belong to England. The interior is the native home of many of our finest flowering plants, like the geraniums and brilliant lilies. Not long ago diamonds were found there; among others, one of the largest ever seen.

Ostrich Farm.

ASIA.

I.—WESTERN ASIA.

Per'-si-a [-*shi-a*]. | **Is-pa-han'** [-*hahn'*]. | **Pal'-es-tine.**
Ar'-a-rat. | **Eu-phra'-tes** [-*fra'-teez*]. | **pome'-gran-ate** [*pum'*-].

1. EAST of Europe and Africa is ASIA, the largest of all the continents. It contains several great and very interesting countries. In the portion nearest to Europe and Africa, which is quite different from the rest of the continent, are *Turkey*, *Arabia*, and *Persia*.

2. TURKEY IN ASIA and Turkey in Europe form one country, called the *Turkish Empire*. This is one of the most interesting regions in the whole world. In the northeastern corner is a little mountain land called *Armenia*, where, some people think, the *Garden of Eden* was. On the border of Armenia is *Ararat*, believed by many to be the mountain on which the ark rested after the flood.

3. From Armenia flow two large rivers,—the *Euphrates* and the *Tigris*, on the banks of which stood the celebrated cities, *Babylon* and *Nineveh*. According to the old writers, they were more magnificent than any cities now in existence; but, strong and great as they were, they have perished, and only heaps of ruins remain to mark the places where they stood.

4. At the east end of the Mediterranean, is *Palestine*,

the country of the Jews. Here was *Jerusalem*, in which Solomon built the magnificent temple; and *Bethlehem*, where Jesus was born. Through a deep valley east of Jerusalem flows the river *Jordan*, in which he was baptized. In this country he lived, and did all the wonderful works recorded of him. The Jordan, not many miles from its source, flows into a basin among the hills, and

Jerusalem.

forms the lovely lake called the *Sea of Galilee*, on the waters of which he so often sailed with his disciples. It is these things which make this land interesting to us.

5. The western part of Turkey is mountainous, but was once very fruitful. On its mountains were forests of cedars; and its valleys and hillsides were covered with vineyards and olive groves, pomegranates and fig trees, mingled with grainfields and rich pas-

tures. Now most of it is quite barren; and in some places are still found the ruins of splendid cities.

6. ARABIA lies beside northern Africa, and is in many respects very different from Turkey. Some parts of it are hot and dry, like the Sahara, — a dreary desert land, dotted with green oases of date palms. Elsewhere there

An Arab Encampment.

are forests of trees yielding rich gums and odors; and in the south, growing upon the hillsides, are groves of the coffee tree, from which the best coffee in the world is obtained.

7. This is the country from which the Arabs came to Africa; and in the dry regions here they lead the same sort of bold, free life, with their herds, their camels, and their swift horses. The horses of Arabia are famous

all over the world for their beauty of form and their fleetness; and the Arab loves his horse as well as he does his wife and children.

8. PERSIA is also a dry country, and the southern part is very warm. In some places you may travel many miles without seeing a single tree, hardly a patch of grass; then suddenly you come in sight of groves of trees, pleasant green fields, and gardens filled with fragrant flowers, in the midst of which is a city. *Ispahan* is such a place. These trees have all been planted by the people in order that they may have wood for burning, and for use in building.

9. Some of these cities have rivers flowing through them; but others are built beside canals, which bring water from some distant lake or river. In this case it sometimes happens that enemies destroy the canal; and then, as there is no water, the people are obliged to remove to some other place. The trees die, the gardens become a desert, and the forsaken city goes to ruin. There are many such ruined cities in Persia.

10. In the mountains which form the borders of Persia are streams and lakes, and fertile valleys which are the native home of many of our finest fruits. Here are great fields of roses, that fill the air with their fragrance, and whole gardens of tulips and many other flowers, carpeting the hillsides with brilliant colors.

11. Groves of peach trees are laden with delicious fruit; and sweet, juicy melons and cucumbers cover the earth. Here, too, strong vines climb from tree to tree, bearing rich grapes, in clusters much larger and heavier than any you have ever seen; and luscious cherries, apricots, and many other fruits grow without care.

II.—THE INDIES.

In'-di-a. | Gan'-ges [-jeez]. | Cal-cut'-ta.

1. East of Arabia, in the southern part of Asia, are two great peninsulas; and a little farther south, in the ocean, is a cluster of the largest islands in the world.

Temples on the Banks of the Ganges.

These peninsulas and islands together are usually called The Indies, though each of them has a separate name.

2. These are all hot countries, with plenty of rain, and are remarkable for the abundance of vegetable and animal productions, as well as for mineral wealth.

3. Almost all the kinds of spices now raised in different parts of the world may be found here in the forests.

There are many rare kinds of wood, rich fruits, and valuable medicines; and from the island of *Java* large quantities of excellent coffee are obtained.

4. Brilliant diamonds, rubies of the finest color, emeralds, and all those stones which are most valued, and used to ornament the crowns of kings and emperors, are found here. For thousands of years other countries all over Asia and Europe have known of the wealth of the Indies, and have sought to obtain these precious things. Many voyages from countries in western Europe, in the time of Columbus, were undertaken in the hope of finding a shorter way to this wonderful land.

5. The greater and more western of the two peninsulas belongs to the government of Great Britain, and is therefore sometimes called *British India*. This is the most interesting of all these countries. In the northern part of this peninsula a large river, called the *Ganges*, flows through a rich plain eastward to the sea.

6. While many of the inhabitants of Europe were scarcely more learned or skillful than are the negroes of Sudan, there were on this plain great cities and splendid temples, books, and learned men. Before any of the great cities now in Europe had been built, the people here knew how to make the finest muslins, rich shawls, and many beautiful things from wood, ivory, pearl, and gold. These were sought for by other nations as much as were the spices and precious stones of the Indies.

7. This plain is still covered with great cities, some of them very old. There are in many of them thousands of English soldiers and merchants, besides all the native people. *Calcutta*, the capital of British India, is in the low, marshy lands, at the mouth of the Ganges.

III.—CHINA AND JAPAN.

| Chi'-na. | Ja-pan'. | To'-ky-o [To'-ke-o]. |
| Can'-ton. | Pe-king'. | Ki-o'-to. |

1. CHINA is in the far eastern part of Asia, bordering upon the Pacific Ocean. The *Empire of Japan* is in the ocean, opposite the northern part of China. In some things these countries are much like our own, having plenty of rain, and being neither very warm, nor too cold for most of the useful plants to grow. But in other things they are very different, as you will see; and they are among the most interesting countries of Asia.

2. China has in the west high mountains, whose tops are covered with snow most of the year. In the east are two broad, rich plains, each having a great river, almost as long as the Mississippi, flowing through it, from the snowy mountains on the west, to the Pacific Ocean at the east.

A Chinese Junk.

Japan is a mountain land, with wide and fertile valleys, and small plains near the sea.

3. The Chinese are a very curious people. They used always to stay in their own country, instead of traveling about all over the world to see and learn, as other people do; and they did not want people from other countries to come and live with them.

4. They did not, for this reason, learn from other nations, and make changes and improvements in their way of doing things, as others do; but for thousands of years they continued to dress, and build their ships and houses, and work, and amuse themselves, just as did their ancestors ages and ages before.

5. They were the first people to find out how to print books, and how to make many useful things; but, while all the other nations of the world have gone on learning, they have not improved, and therefore are much behind them. Now they are finding out that they are not the wisest people in the world, and have begun to change their ways.

6. In no other country of the same size will you find so many people living as in China. Every foot of land is turned to account. Even hills and mountain sides, which are so steep that the earth would all be washed away by the rain, have little walls of stone built across them to hold the soil, so that they look like a very broad flight of stairs.

7. These steps, or *terraces*, are carefully cultivated, and made to produce the useful crops of the country. They are watered by hand, and thus much work is needed to raise plants in some parts of China. Even on the rivers are floating gardens, made by putting earth on rafts, or floors of timber. On these are little houses, in which the people live, and float about from place to place.

8. Nearly the same things grow in China and Japan. The chief productions are rice, cotton, wheat, the mulberry, and, most important of all, the *tea plant*. Nearly all the tea which is used in the world is raised in these two countries, and the Indies.

9. For ages the Chinese have fed the silkworm, and manufactured silk; and have also made porcelain cups and saucers, and other things for the table, as well as vases and ornaments of many kinds. These are called "China ware;" because, for a very long time, the people of China alone knew how to make them. Thus you see that they must be very industrious; for they make all these beautiful things with their own hands, and not by machinery, as they are made in our country and in Europe.

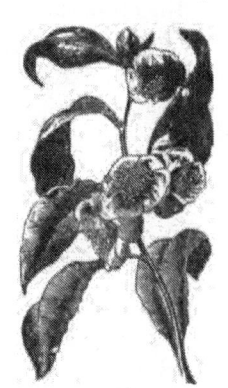

Tea Plant.

10. Both the Chinese and Japanese are yellowish-brown people; but they are much more cultivated than any of the other nations of their color. After standing still for ages, however, the Japanese, unlike the Chinese, have adopted within the last fifty years many of the inventions of western civilization, and Japan is now in consequence by far the most progressive and the strongest nation of Asia.

11. Both these countries have many great, old, and interesting cities. *Peking*, in China, has a high, strong wall around it, with gates that are always guarded during the day, and kept shut and barred at night, so that no enemy can come in. It has also large beautiful

gardens, with hills, lakes, and groves, besides palaces for the emperor and his relations.

12. *Canton* was for many years the only city of China which the emperor would allow ships from other countries to visit. The emperor of Japan and his ministers live in *Tokyo*. *Kioto* is also an important city.

IV.—MIDDLE ASIA AND SIBERIA.

Him-a'-la-ya [*Him-äh'-*]. | **Kash-mir'**. | **Ti-bet'**.

1. NORTH of India, is a great wall of mountains, called the *Himalaya*, "*the home of the snows.*" They are the highest mountains in the whole world, and the most steep and wild. It is almost impossible to cross them at any place, because they are so very steep; and, besides, there are terrible storms, which cover the way with snow, so that a traveler would not know where to find a safe path.

2. The rivers here flow very swiftly, and fill the air with mists and dampness; and the valleys are only gorges, often so deep and narrow that the sun never shines at the bottom of them. Away up in this great home of the snows, you will not see a single animal, nor hear any living thing; and all is so wild and solemn, that even the sound of your own steps will make you tremble.

3. On the middle slopes of the mountains, are many plants and animals like those on the Alps. Above the forests the mountain sides are covered with bright-colored Alpine flowers; and many interesting plants

and animals are natives of these heights. This is the home of the beautiful *horse-chestnut* tree which we plant in our streets and gardens. In one of the valleys, called the *Vale of Kashmir* (or *Cashmere*), the cashmere goat lives, from whose wool the elegant shawls of India are made.

4. South of this range is British India, with its spice forests, its great animals, and continual summer. Beyond it, to the north, is a vast mountain land, so elevated that even the bottoms of the valleys are nearly as high as the top of the Alps; while the peaks rising far above them are almost as high as the Himalaya.

5. This mountain land is *Tibet*. It is the highest and most mountainous country in the world. Some of the lower valleys are populous and fertile.

In the Himalaya Mountains.

6. In summer the mountain pastures are full of flocks of sheep and goats, famous for their fine silky wool, from which handsome cloth and shawls are made. In

winter the whole country is very cold,—so cold that travelers are often frozen to death on their journeys.

7. Beyond the snowy mountains, on the northern border of Tibet, is a broad, barren table-land. In the western, lowest part, are streams and lakes, and villages and cities, green pastures, and cultivated fields.

A Scene in Mongolia.

8. This is *Mongolia*. At times one may see this almost desert country covered with great herds of horses, oxen, goats, sheep, and camels. Low tents are grouped in the midst of them; and men on swift horses ride about, watching the herds, and at night gathering them all together close to the tents. But in a day or two all are gone; and only the naked, dreary land is left, with not a plant, nor a living animal, to be seen.

9. The *Mongols* wander over the table-land, wherever they can find food for the herds, frequently remaining only a few days in the same place. They are a very warlike people; and often great companies of them come suddenly upon some of the villages in the better part of the table-land, rob and kill the people, burn the houses, and dash away again, before any one can punish them.

10. Farther north, a great country, called *Siberia*, which belongs to Russia, extends entirely across Asia, from east to west. This, like the northern part of Russia, contains a forest country, at the north of which are great plains, without trees, and covered with snow and ice nearly all the year. In the south there are rich gold mines, and valleys and plains, where there might be fine farms if there were people to cultivate them. But most of the Russians living in Siberia work the mines, and the natives of the country wander from place to place with herds of reindeer.

11. Journeys are made across this country, from Peking in China to St. Petersburg in Russia; and tea, silk, furs, and many other things, are carried this immense distance. A large part of the Russians in Siberia are exiles, who were sent there by the government for some offense committed in their own country.

THE INDIAN OCEAN AND AUSTRALIA.

Aus-tra'-li-a. | Mur'-ray. | kan-ga-roo' [kang-].

1. THE INDIAN OCEAN is south of Asia, and must be crossed in going from Asia or from Africa to Australia. Terrible hurricanes often occur on this ocean. One may be sailing in the morning with a pleasant breeze and clear sky, when suddenly he sees a small black cloud on the horizon. Soon it spreads, until it covers the whole sky, the thunder begins to roll, and the lightning flashes at every moment.

2. A terrific wind strikes the ship, the rain falls in torrents, and great waves rise like mountains of water. They dash themselves on the shore with a terrible roaring, covering it with the broken timbers of wrecked ships, and filling the air with white foam.

3. In parts of this ocean, there is a kind of oyster within whose shell are found the beautiful pearls worn by ladies in necklaces and other ornaments. These can be obtained only by diving, and seeking the oyster at the bottom of the sea, a very difficult and dangerous work.

4. AUSTRALIA is the smallest of the continents, being only about the size of the United States. It is south of Asia, and a long way from it; but the great islands of the Indies make a sort of bridge between them. The

most populous part of Australia is the southeast. Here are low mountains in which large quantities of gold are found; and a broad, rich plain, with a fine river, called the *Murray*, flowing through it.

5. There are some things very curious about Australia. What would you think of seeing animals like the kangaroo, which, instead of walking squarely on four feet, as others do, goes hopping about on the tail and the two long hind legs? And what would you think of seeing a forest of trees whose tough bark splits and falls off every year, instead of the leaves; and of others, covered with leaves, yet making not much more shadow than if they had none, because the edge of the leaf is toward the light?

Kangaroo and Lyre Bird.

6. When white people first went to this continent, they found hardly any plants which they could use for food. But seeds have been taken there from other countries; and now fields of wheat and corn and other grains, with orchards of peaches, pears, apples, and other fruits, grow in many parts. There are also plantations of cotton; but there are not enough farmers to plow and plant all the rich plain, and therefore much of it is used for the pasturage of sheep and cattle.

THE PACIFIC OCEAN.

mul'-ti-tudes. | vol-ca'-noes. | Whit'-sun-day.

1. THE PACIFIC, which separates Asia and Australia from North and South America, is the largest of all the oceans. It covers nearly half of the surface of the globe with one vast expanse of water. In different parts of it are multitudes of islands, besides the great ones near the continents. Many contain high mountains; and some were built up by volcanoes throwing out substances from within the earth.

2. But there are islands of still another sort in the Pacific Ocean. You may be sailing through the warm part of it, with nothing in sight but the broad blue waters and the sky, when presently you will discover, rising out of the sea before you, a grove of tall green palm trees. It is very strange to see them there, for they appear to be growing directly from the waves. But when you are nearer, you find that they stand on a flat island just high enough to prevent being overflowed.

3. Under the palms the ground is covered with plants of the richest green, and between them and the waves is a broad beach of sand as white as snow. Presently you see that what seemed to be only a long narrow island is a complete ring, with palm trees on all parts

THE PACIFIC OCEAN. 183

of it, and within, a clear, still lake of the blue sea water. Such is *Whitsunday* Island. The Pacific has many of these flat islands, though not many just like this.

4. The ships on the Pacific are nearly all from the United States and countries of Europe. They are going to China, India, Japan, and Australia, or returning with tea, coffee, and spices, silk, pearls, and gold. The island peoples of the Pacific have small odd-looking vessels, in which they go from place to place along their own coasts, but do not venture far out into the wide sea. If we sail across the Pacific

Whitsunday Island.

from the strange shores of Asia and Australia, we can reach our own country.

5. You have now visited all the most important countries of the world. You have seen no two which are quite alike, but something interesting or pleasant has met you everywhere. You have learned just enough of the great earth to make you wish to know more; and you will find a few important things, which you will be glad to learn, in PART SECOND.

THE CHILD'S WORLD.

Great, wide, beautiful, wonderful World,
With the wonderful water round you curled,
And the wonderful grass upon your breast, —
World, you are beautifully drest.

The wonderful air is over me,
And the wonderful wind is shaking the tree:
It walks on the water, and whirls the mills,
And talks to itself on the top of the hills.

You, friendly Earth! how far do you go
With the wheat fields that nod and the rivers that flow,
With cities and gardens, and cliffs and isles,
And people upon you for thousands of miles?

Ah, you are so great, and I am so small,
I tremble to think of you, World, at all;
And yet, when I said my prayers to-day,
A whisper inside me seemed to say, —

"You are more than the Earth, though you are such a dot;
You can love and think, and the Earth cannot."

"Lilliput Lectures."

PART II.
GEOGRAPHICAL PRIMER.

TO THE TEACHER.

It will be observed that each lesson in Part II. consists of three distinct divisions. The INTRODUCTION serves to recall previously acquired ideas connected with the topic of the lesson, and to awaken interest in what follows. It should be carefully read, not memorized; and the teacher should call attention to any important points.

The large print is the lesson proper, which is to be memorized and recited in the usual way. The words in **boldface** indicate the leading idea of each paragraph. In the reviews, are questions upon the lessons which the teacher can use in recitation if desired.

The EXERCISE is not a part of the lesson, to be studied beforehand, but only suggests a familiar talk between teacher and pupils after the recitation, such as all primary teachers are more or less accustomed to. The pupils are questioned to test their general comprehension of the subject treated. The geographical names used in the lesson are found on the map, so that the succeeding *Map Lesson* is made easy; and items of information are given, calculated to interest the pupils or to fix in mind the facts of the lesson. In short, this is the teacher's opportunity for oral instruction; and it may be extended at discretion, especially with reference to local or home geography.

The MAP LESSONS are to be recited from a wall map, a blackboard map, or with no map in view, according to the judgment of the teacher. The WRITTEN EXERCISES and REVIEWS occurring at frequent intervals add variety, and will be found of great value.

By means of the Readings in Part I., bearing upon the subjects of successive lessons, and the variety of work presented in Part II., a constant interest will be maintained in classes, and the happiest results may be expected.

INTRODUCTION.

I.—THE EARTH.

(Part I., Pages 1-3.)

In the preceding part of the book, you have been reading, making imaginary journeys all over the world. In this part, are lessons about the most important countries, to be studied and learned by heart. This is a different kind of work; but you will find it just as pleasant, for you wish to become wise, and every lesson will help you a little in gaining a knowledge of the great world.

The **earth** is the world on which we live.

The **shape** of the earth is round, like an orange.

The **size** of the earth is so great that to go round it one must travel two hundred and fifty miles a day, for one hundred days.

The **surface** of the earth is composed of land and water.

The **water** covers nearly three quarters of the surface. The whole water surface is called the **sea**. It is divided into **oceans**.

A Globe.

The **land** forms about one quarter of the surface.

It is divided into large masses, called **continents,** and small bodies, called **islands.**

EXERCISE.— How far is it round the earth? How many weeks are there in the hundred days spent in going round it? How many months? Do you see more land, or more water, on the earth? How do people make the land useful? What use is made of the sea? Would you think there would be more sea than land? Why do you think so? If there were three parts of land to one part of water, the land would be much less pleasant than it is. Some time you will understand this. The picture in this lesson shows you the shape of the earth. The two dark, rough-looking places represent continents; the rest, oceans.

II.—REPRESENTATIONS OF THE EARTH.

It is not very easy to learn how the continents and oceans are situated on the earth, nor where the different countries are, unless there is some way of showing these things to

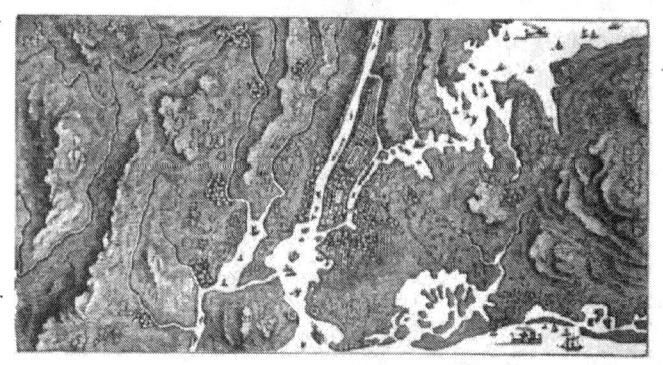

Balloon View of New York and Vicinity.

our eyes. For this reason people have contrived ways of representing the earth, to help in learning geography.

REPRESENTATIONS OF THE EARTH. 189

The earth is **represented** both by globes and maps.

A **globe** is a ball with drawings upon it, to represent the continents and oceans as they appear on the earth.

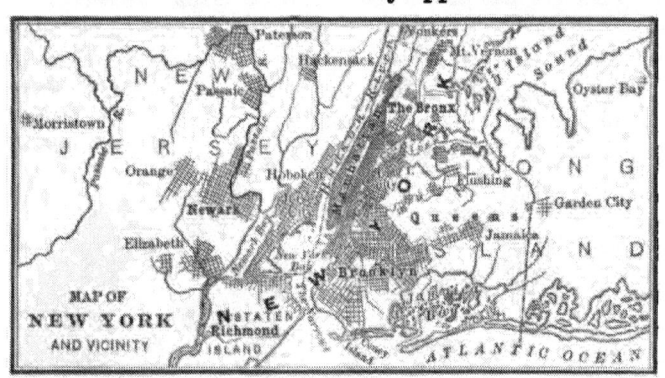

Map of New York and Vicinity

A **map** is a drawing which represents any part of the surface of the earth.

A **hemisphere map** represents one half of the earth's surface.

The **colors** on the large maps in this book show how the land is divided into continents, and the continents into countries.

EXERCISE. — Here is a view of New York and the country around it, as one would see it looking down from a balloon. There are besides the great city, the smaller cities scattered about, the river, the bay, the ocean, and the islands. Next comes a *map* of the same country. It does not show any of these things as they look in nature, but has only lines and marks to stand for them, with a name beside each to show what it represents. Which is prettier to look at, — the balloon view or the map? What can you learn from the map which the view does not show? Read the names of all the objects represented on this map. Which city have you read about? Which river? What can you remember about them? Can you make a map of your schoolroom? Try it.

III.—DIRECTION ON MAPS AND GLOBES.

Map makers put on the globe and on maps, two sets of lines to enable us to see the direction of places and countries from each other, as well as their location. They are north-and-south lines, and east-and-west lines. On the globe, as the picture of the hemispheres shows, the north-and-south lines all meet in two points.

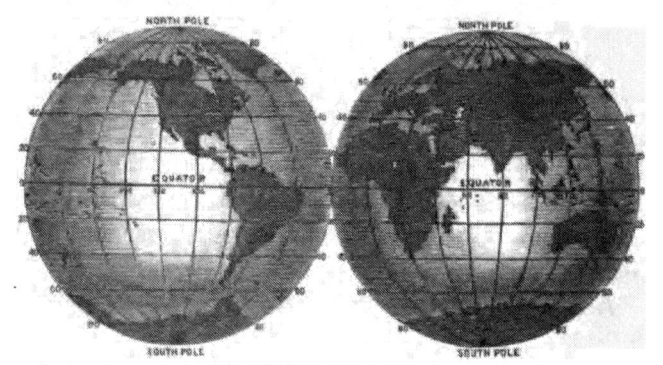

The Earth in Hemispheres.

Directions are shown on maps and globes by two sets of lines crossing each other.

North-and-south lines cross the map from top to bottom, and are called **meridians.**

On the globe the meridians all meet in two points, the **north pole** and the **south pole.**

The east-and-west lines cross the map from side to side, and are called **parallels.**

The line extending around the globe, half way between the poles, is the **equator.**

Toward the top of the map, along a meridian, is **north**; toward the bottom, **south.**

Toward the right hand, along a parallel, is **east**; toward the left, **west**.

EXERCISE. — Turn to the hemisphere maps (pp. 194, 195). What continents are shown upon each? What oceans? Find the equator; the meridians; the parallels. Trace a line directly north and south across the map. Trace a line directly east and west. In what direction is Europe from Asia? Asia from Australia? Africa from Europe? Australia from Europe? Africa from Asia? South America from North America? On p. 190 is a picture of the hemispheres: find in it the meridians; the parallels; the north pole; the south pole; the equator. Can you tell the names of the continents and oceans in the picture?

IV. — DISTANCE ON MAPS AND GLOBES.

Distance on maps and globes is shown by numbers upon the parallels and meridians. You know that along some railroads you see mileposts, from time to time, with numbers upon them giving the distance in miles from some important place.

But on globes and maps distances are marked in *degrees*, not miles. A degree (written 1°) is one three hundred and sixtieth part of the whole distance around the earth. Degrees north or south are always reckoned from the equator. Degrees east or west are reckoned from some meridian agreed upon, which is named the *prime meridian*.

Distance from the equator is called **latitude**. Places north of the equator are in **north latitude**; those south, in **south latitude**.

Distance from the prime meridian is called **longitude**. Places east of the prime meridian are in **east longitude**; those west, in **west longitude**.

Each **parallel** is marked with the number of degrees of latitude between it and the equator.

Each **meridian** is marked with the number of degrees of longitude between it and the prime meridian.

The **equator** and the **prime meridian** are marked 0, because they are the lines from which reckoning begins.

EXERCISE. — Turn to the map of the eastern hemisphere. What figure is against the equator, in the border of this map? Find the meridian marked 0. Why are these two lines marked 0? Read the numbers on the meridians east of the prime meridian. Read the numbers on the parallels north of the equator. What do these numbers show? Is North America in east, or west, longitude? Is it in north, or south, latitude?

V. — REVIEW.

I. What is the shape of the earth? How large is it? Of what does its surface consist? How much of it is land? How much is water? What is the whole water surface called? How is the water divided? How is the land divided? What is geography?

II. How is the earth represented for study? What is a globe? What is a map? What do the hemisphere maps show? What are the colors on the maps for?

III. How is direction shown on maps? What are the north-and-south lines called? The east-and-west lines? Where do the meridians meet? Where is the equator? Which way on the map is north? East? South? West?

IV. How is distance shown on maps? What is a degree? What is latitude? North latitude? South latitude? What is longitude? East longitude? West longitude? What does the number on each parallel show? On each meridian? How are the equator and the prime meridian marked? Why?

VI. — CONTINENTS, ISLANDS, AND OCEANS.

You have already noticed how the sea is divided into oceans, and the land into continents and islands. You will see on the globe that all the great islands are near the borders of the continents; but there are very many little ones far away in the midst of the oceans. The continents and islands contain countries, and are the homes of people. The oceans afford routes of travel and trade between the countries on their borders.

There are **six continents.** Europe, Asia, Africa, and Australia are in the eastern hemisphere; North America and South America, in the western.

The **largest continent** is Asia, but Europe and North America have the *richest* and *most important countries.*

The **largest islands** are New Guinea and Borneo, between Asia and Australia; but the richest and most powerful is Great Britain, near the coast of Europe.

There are **five oceans.** The Pacific is the *largest.* All the most important countries border on the *Atlantic* or its arms, and the most travel and trade cross it. The others are the *Indian, Arctic,* and *Antarctic* Oceans.

EXERCISE. — Turn to the hemisphere maps. What continents, in each hemisphere, border upon the Pacific Ocean? The Atlantic Ocean? What continents border upon the Indian Ocean? The Arctic? The Antarctic? Which of all these oceans border upon our own country? Which ocean do we use most? What use do we make of it?

The girls may write what we would see in crossing the Atlantic; the boys write how, where, and for what, whales are caught. (Pages 110–112.)

WESTERN HEMISPHERE.

What continents are in the western hemisphere?
What oceans are partly in the western hemisphere?
In which continent is the United States?

In what direction from us is South America?
In what direction from South America are we?
In what direction from us is each of the oceans?
Which continent is crossed by the equator?
Is North America in north latitude, or in south latitude? **Why?**

EASTERN HEMISPHERE.

What continents are in the eastern hemisphere?
What ocean is wholly in this hemisphere? What ones partly?
What continent is crossed by the equator?

Which continents are in north latitude?
In what latitude is most of Africa?
In what latitude is Australia?
In what direction from Europe is Asia? Africa? Australia?
What oceans touch Europe? Asia? Africa? Australia?

VII.—BORDER LANDS AND WATERS.

When you notice the map of North America, you see that a very crooked line marks its borders. In some places the land juts out into the ocean, so that parts of it are nearly

1. Mountain. 2. Plain. 3. Island. 4. Cape. 5. Peninsula.
6. Bay. 7. Harbor. 8. River. 9. Strait.

separated from the rest. In other places, parts of the oceans run into the land so that they seem almost like lakes. There are small points of land here and there, and there is a long narrow neck connecting North America with South America.

The land which borders upon the water is called the **coast** or **shore**.

A **peninsula** is a part of the coast land nearly surrounded by water.

A **cape** is a point of land projecting into the water.

An **isthmus** is a narrow neck of land connecting two bodies of land.

Parts of the oceans which lie within or among the lands are called **gulfs, bays,** and **seas.**

Narrow passages of water, connecting bodies of water, are called **straits, channels,** and **sounds.** The shallow passages are the ones usually called sounds.

EXERCISE.— Turn to the map of North America (p. 243). Point to any part of the coast. Name all the gulfs, bays, and seas which you find along the coast. What straits can you find? What waters does each connect? What isthmus can you find? What lands does it connect? Name all the capes which you see; the peninsulas; the islands. Name the lands and waters in the picture opposite. What harbor (p. 40) have you read about? Where is New York Harbor?

VIII.—LAND SURFACE.
(PART I., PAGES 20, 65, 66.)

In parts of our country, we have seen wide plains, some with a level surface, and some covered with low hills. Elsewhere the land is lifted up into great mountain ranges with valleys between them; or it forms wide table-lands so dry as to be almost deserts. All these different lands are useful. Some are good for tillage and pasturage, some afford fine forests, and others contain rich minerals.

Hills are parts of the land but little higher than the surrounding country. **Mountains** are very high lands.

A long ridge of mountain land is a **mountain range.**
Many ranges connected make **a mountain system.**

A **valley** is a narrow tract of land between higher lands.

A **plain** is an extended region of level land. Some plains are quite flat, others have a rolling surface.

A high plain is called a **table-land,** or **plateau.** Some table-lands are surrounded by mountains.

EXERCISE. — What plains in the United States have you read about? What mountains do you remember? Find these on the map (p. 243) of North America. Do you remember the highest mountains in the world (p. 176)? The highest peak is Mount Everest, more than five and one half miles high. What kinds of land are shown in the picture on p. 7? 16? 30? 47?

IX.—THE WATER UPON THE LAND.

(PART I., PAGES 23-29.)

You know that some of the rain, as it falls, sinks into the ground, and makes springs. Brooks flow from springs, making rivers and lakes; and rivers find their way from the highlands, through the valleys and across the plains, to the sea. Did you know that the water is only seeking its own home? That which feeds the springs, and makes the lakes and streams, once rose from the sea as vapor, and floated away over the land to produce rain clouds. This is one benefit that comes from the fact that there is more sea than land on the earth, for so the land gets more moisture.

A **spring** is water flowing from within the ground. Springs are the sources of brooks and rivers.

Brooks are small streams of water; **rivers** are large streams.

THE WATER UPON THE LAND. 199

Tributaries are the streams which flow into a river.

Towards the source, or beginning, is **up** stream; and towards the opposite end, or *mouth*, is **down** stream.

The **banks** of a stream are the ground along each side of it. The **right** bank is the one on the right hand

Lake Hopatcong.

of a person facing down stream. The other one is the **left** bank.

A **lake** is a **body** of water in a hollow of the land. Most lakes are fresh, but some are salt like the sea.

EXERCISE. — Turn to the map of North America (p. 243). Find Lake Superior; some other great lakes. How are they represented? Find the Mississippi River. How are rivers represented? What other rivers can you find? Where is the source of the Missouri? Where does the water of the Missouri find the ocean?

X.—REVIEW.

VI. How many continents are there? Name those in each hemisphere. Which is the largest? Which have the most important countries? (See p. 193.) What and where are the largest two islands? What and where is the most rich and powerful island? How many oceans are there? Name them. Which is the largest? Which is most important? Why is the Atlantic important?

VII. What is the coast? A peninsula? A cape? An isthmus? What are parts of the ocean extending into the land called? What are narrow passages of water called? How do the sounds differ from other passages of water?

VIII. What are hills? Mountains? What is a mountain range? A mountain system? A valley? A plain? A tableland? What kinds of surface have plains? What is the highest mountain system in the world? What is the highest peak? How high is it?

IX. What is a spring? A brook? A river? A tributary stream? A lake? What is meant by up stream? Down stream? What is the source of a stream? The mouth? The banks? The right and the left bank? What kind of water is in lakes?

Write all you remember about the Mississippi,—where its source is, what great tributaries it has, and what sort of country is along its course.

XI.—CLIMATE AND ZONES.

(PART I., PAGES 78-80, 92, 99.)

On the Amazon, you know, there is constant summer. Our country has summer during a part of the year, and winter about as long. The Arctic shores have winter nearly all the time. Some countries have a moist air, and others are very dry; while in some the air is so impure as to make people sick. In describing these conditions, we use the word *climate*. South America has a *hot climate*, our country has a *temperate climate,* and the Arctic shores have a *cold climate.* Countries alike in climate are situated about the same distance from the equator; so we think of them as forming belts, or *zones,* around the earth. There are four parallels, with names, which mark the boundaries of the zones.

The **climate** of a country is the state of the air. It may be warm, cold, or **temperate**; moist or dry; healthy or unhealthy.

The hottest countries lie on and near the equator, and form the **Torrid** (burning) **Zone**. It extends from the tropic of Cancer to the tropic of Capricorn.

The temperate countries form **two Temperate Zones**. The northern extends from the tropic of Cancer to the Arctic circle; the southern, from the tropic of Capricorn to the Antarctic circle.

The very cold regions form **two Frigid** (frozen) **Zones**. The northern extends from the Arctic circle to the north pole; the southern, from the Antarctic circle to the south pole.

EXERCISE.—Turn to the map of hemispheres. Find the equator and the four named parallels. In which zone is our country? Most of Africa? Of South America? Of Europe and Asia? Which zones have most land? Which zone has least? In which would you rather live? Why? What climate is there at the foot (p. 99) of the Andes? On their middle slopes? At the top? Climate always grows cooler from the bottom to the top of mountains, as well as from the equator towards the poles.

XII.—THE PLANTS AND ANIMALS.
(PART I., PAGES 93-97.)

Nowhere are there such great forests, such brilliant flowers, so many choice fruits and rich spices, as in the silvas of the

Amazon and in the Indies. The Torrid Zone has no winter to stop the growth of plants, but plenty of heat and moisture to perfect them. Beyond this zone, plants become fewer and less luxuriant until, in the Frigid Zone, there are hardly any but mosses. The Torrid Zone, too, has the largest and most dangerous wild beasts and serpents, and the most brilliant birds and insects. In the Temperate Zone most of the wild animals are harmless, many of the birds sing, and a few insects are poisonous.

The Zones.

Plants grow most luxuriantly in the Torrid Zone. Coffee, sugar cane, spices, and many delicate fruits belong to this zone.

In the **Temperate Zone** plants stop growing in winter, and most trees lose their leaves. Most of the cultivated plants are native to the North Temperate Zone.

The **Frigid Zone** has few plants except mosses.

Wild animals are most numerous, largest, and most dangerous in the Torrid Zone, and the birds and insects are most brilliant.

The **domestic animals** nearly all originated in the North Temperate Zone.

The **Frigid Zone** has few large land animals, but the greatest creatures of the sea are found there.

EXERCISE. — The picture on the opposite page shows some plants and animals in the different zones. Name some in the Torrid Zone. Have you seen any of these, or any others of that zone? What animals of our country have you seen most? Do you see any of them in the picture? In what zone are they? Because they are tamed, and accustomed to live among men, they are called *domestic* animals. What animals do you see in the South Temperate Zone? In the Frigid Zones? What makes the Torrid Zone best for plants?

XIII. — RACES OF MEN.

In our country, are white men and negroes, reddish-brown Indians, and a few yellowish-brown Chinese and Japanese. On the islands of the Pacific, are blackish-brown people, and in Australia black people. On account of such differences among them, men are divided into *races*.

There are six **races** of men, — one white, three brownish, and two black.

The **white race** are the native people of Europe and western Asia; but they have spread over America and parts of the other continents. This is the most powerful race, and has made most improvement.

GEOG. READ. & PRIM. — 14

The **yellowish-brown** people belong to Japan, China, and the rest of eastern Asia. They are called the *yellow*, or *Mongolian*, race.

The **blackish-brown** people live on the islands of the Pacific. They are called the *brown* race, or *Malays*.

The **reddish-brown**, or copper-colored people, are the Indians of America. They are called the *red* race.

James Russell Lowell.

The **black races** belong to Africa and Australia. The first negroes of our country came from Africa.

EXERCISE. — You have seen persons belonging to the white race. What other races have you seen? Think of one person of each race that you have seen, and write all about him. Tell whether he is a large or a small person, the color of his skin and eyes, what sort of hair he has, anything singular about the shape of his head and features, and what sort of dress he wears.

XIV. — CIVILIZED MEN.
(PART I., PAGES 60-63.)

In our country, in Europe, and in other parts of the world, are states, kingdoms, and empires, with rich cities and educated people who busy themselves about many different occupations. These are *civilized* nations.

In Africa, and some other countries, are men who get all their food and clothing from the wild plants and animals, and know how to build only the rudest huts for shelter. These are *savages*. In still other countries the people till the soil, or raise cattle, instead of supplying their wants only from wild plants and animals. They build better houses, and know how to make many things; but they have neither books nor schools for the improvement of their minds. Such are *barbarous* people.

Commerce.

Civilized men supply their wants chiefly by **agriculture, manufacturing,** and **commerce.**

In countries on the seacoast, they also engage in *fishing;* where there are forests, in *lumbering;* and where there are valuable beds of stone or other minerals, in *quarrying* and *mining.*

Agriculture is tilling the soil, and raising plants and animals, to procure materials for food and clothing.

Manufacturing is making articles from raw materials. Most things obtained by agriculture must be manufactured before they are fit for use.

Commerce is buying and selling, or exchanging goods. Some countries can better produce one thing, and some another. By commerce, each can obtain the productions of all.

EXERCISE. — These are but few of the things civilized people do. Name some classes of persons who do other things. (Artists, who spend their time in making beautiful things; preachers and teachers, who instruct the people; lawyers, doctors, authors, etc.) Name the materials we use most for food; for clothing; for shelter. How do we get them? Name some of the things we obtain only by commerce. From what countries do they come? What business is shown in the picture on the preceding page? On p. 30? 36? 49? Which business would you prefer? Why? The pictures on pp. 64, 81, and 165 show savage life. Would you like it?

XV.—REVIEW.

XI. What is climate? How many zones are there? Where is the Torrid Zone? Each Temperate Zone? Each Frigid Zone? How does climate change from the equator to the poles? From the bottom to the top of mountains?

XII. In what zone are plants most luxuriant? In what zones least so? To what zone do most of our cultivated plants belong? Where are wild animals largest and most dangerous? In which were the domestic animals native? What sort of animals live in the Frigid Zone?

XIII. How many races are there? What are their colors? Where is the white race? The yellow race? The brown race? The red race? Where are the black races?

XIV. How do civilized nations supply their wants? Define agriculture; manufacturing; commerce. How do savages supply their wants? Barbarous people?

NORTH AMERICA.

XVI.—THE UNITED STATES.

(Part I., Pages 8-12, 17-19, 63-69.)

In imaginary journeys we crossed the Atlantic Plain in New Jersey, seeing its fine farms; and the Appalachian Mountains in Pennsylvania, noticing the abundance of iron and coal; then we entered the rich, rolling Central Plain in

A Western Farm.

Ohio. We descended the Mississippi, passing prairie farms, cotton fields, and sugar plantations. We crossed the Rocky Mountains, the barren table-land, and the Sierra Nevadas, with their treasures of gold and silver, and through wide, fruitful valleys, we reached the Pacific.

The **United States** is in the middle part of North America. It extends from the Atlantic to the Pacific, and from the Great Lakes to the Gulf of Mexico.

The **Atlantic Plain** is on the eastern side, bordering upon the Atlantic Ocean.

The **Appalachian Mountains** lie next, extending from the northern boundary nearly to the southern.

The **Central Plain** fills the middle, reaching from the Appalachian to the Rocky Mountains.

The **table-land** and the **mountain systems** that form its borders occupy the western part of the country. Beyond them are only valleys and low coast ranges.

EXERCISE. — (Open books to map of United States.) Across what three States (pp. 8, 12, 20) were our first journeys? Find these States. Find the cities noticed in them. How (see United States map, left-hand lower corner) are the cities marked on the map? Why, then, is Trenton marked differently from Cincinnati? What region is between the Appalachian and the Rocky Mountains? The Central Plain is the richest division of our country: it is also the largest. Write all you remember about the surface of the Central Plain.

XVII.—CLIMATE OF THE UNITED STATES.
(PART I., PAGES 10, 33-37.)

You know how much warmer the southern part of our country is than the northern. The southernmost points reach nearly to the tropic, and are almost as warm as the Torrid Zone. But the western half is very unlike the eastern in moisture. You remember how productive the country is throughout the east, how dry it becomes towards the Rocky Mountains, and how barren the table-land is. But beyond the Sierra Nevada and Cascade Mountains are rich valleys, with plenty of **rain**.

The **United States** is in the southern half of the North Temperate Zone.

The **climate** of the northern border is cool, winter lasting several months. Towards the south it becomes warmer, and the southern border has hardly any winter.

Rain is abundant in the eastern half of the country, but much of the high land in the western half is naturally quite dry. The Pacific coast lands have rain enough, and are warmer than the Atlantic coasts.

The cultivated **plants** vary with the climate, — wheat growing to the extreme north. Farther south are corn, tobacco, and the vine; then cotton and rice; and, in the southernmost parts, sugar cane, figs, and oranges.

EXERCISE. — (Open books to map of United States.) Name the northern divisions of the country west of Lake Huron; the northernmost State on the Atlantic coast. What parallel crosses these divisions? Where is this parallel on the globe? (Half way from the equator to the north pole.) Name the two southernmost States. What parallel is near their southern points? Find the southernmost point of California. What city on the Atlantic coast is just opposite this? You see that the Pacific coast is opposite the middle and northern part of the Atlantic coast, but it is as warm as the middle and southern part. Find the meridian of 100° west longitude; all the dry, barren lands lie west of it.

XVIII. — DIVISIONS OF THE UNITED STATES.

The eastern half of the United States contains a much larger population than the western. Near the Rocky Mountains and on most of the table-land beyond, the ground is naturally too dry to produce enough to support a population; and the water needed for the growth of plants must be brought from long distances with great trouble. Hence, at first, not many people went to these high lands, except where gold and silver could be obtained. The Territories are great divisions of country which do not yet contain people enough to make States.

The United States is **divided** into forty-six States and four Territories (besides its island possessions in the West Indies and in the Pacific).

Fourteen of these **States** border on the Atlantic Ocean, three on the Pacific Ocean, and five on the Gulf of Mexico.

The **Territories** are Alaska, Hawaii, Arizona, and New Mexico. The Territories of Alaska and Hawaii are situated outside of the main part of the United States.

The **District of Columbia,** in which Washington is situated, belongs to the government.

EXERCISE.—(Open books to map of United States.) Read the names of the Territories. Read the names of all the States that touch the Atlantic; the Gulf of Mexico; the Pacific; the Mississippi; the Missouri; the Ohio. What other States are there? Copy the names of all the States.

XIX.—GOVERNMENT OF THE UNITED STATES.

In the United States the rulers and law makers of the nation are all chosen by the people. Such a government is a *Republic*. The highest officer is the *President*. There are two bodies of men, who unite to make the laws. They are together called the *Congress;* one body is the *Senate,* and the other is the *House of Representatives*.

Every State sends two of its citizens to the Senate, and one or more to the House; and every State takes part in choosing the President, so that all have a share in govern-

GOVERNMENT OF THE UNITED STATES. 211

ing the country. The President lives at Washington, and Congress meets there; thus it is the *seat* of government.

The United States is a **republic**. It contains over sixty millions of people. The President is the highest officer of the government.

Faneuil Hall, Boston, — the Old "Cradle of Liberty."

The **laws** are made by Congress, which meets every year. **Congress** consists of a Senate and a House of Representatives.

The **Senate** is composed of two **senators** from each State.

The **House** consists of **representatives** from each

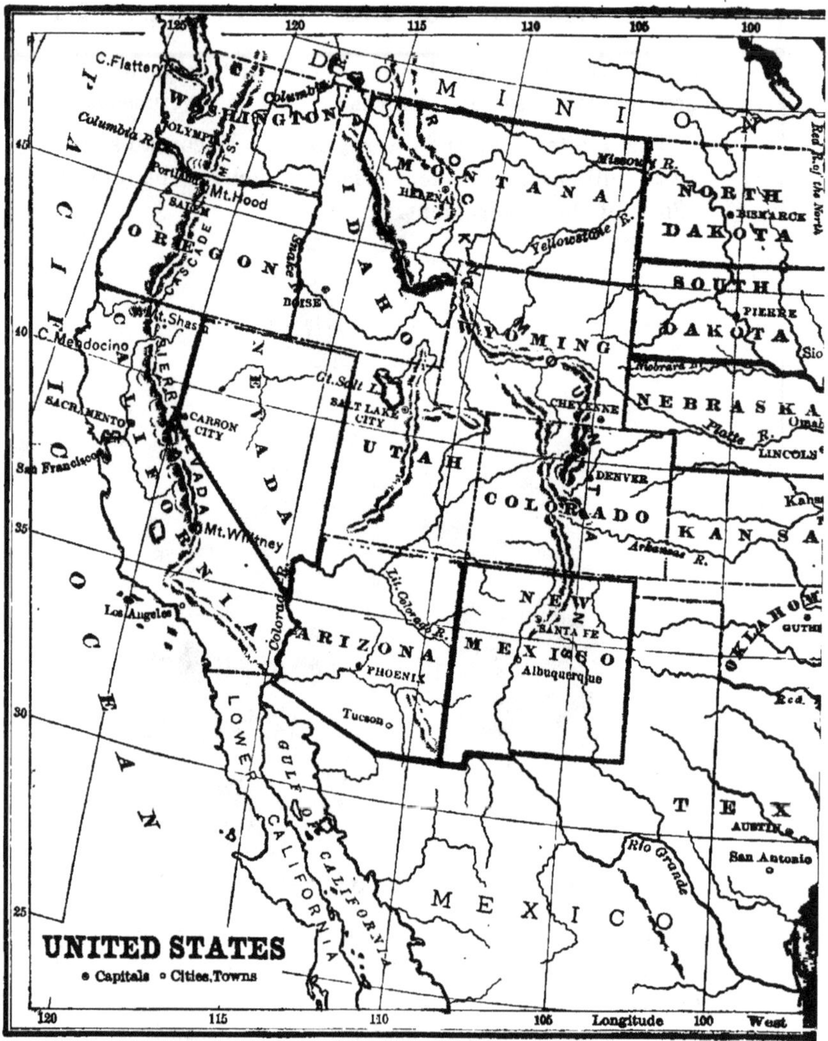
UNITED STATES
Capitals
Cities, Towns
DOMINION
PACIFIC OCEAN
WASHINGTON
OREGON
CALIFORNIA
NEVADA
IDAHO
MONTANA
WYOMING
UTAH
COLORADO
ARIZONA
NEW MEXICO
NORTH DAKOTA
SOUTH DAKOTA
NEBRASKA
KANSA
TEX
MEXICO
LOWER CALIFORNIA
GULF OF CALIFORNIA
C. Flattery
Columbia R.
Portland
Mt. Hood
SALEM
BOISE
Snake R.
Mt. Shasta
C. Mendocino
SACRAMENTO
San Francisco
CARSON CITY
Mt. Whitney
Los Angeles
Colorado R.
Gt. Salt L.
SALT LAKE CITY
HELENA
Missouri R.
Yellowstone R.
BISMARCK
PIERRE
CHEYENNE
Nebraska R.
Platte R.
LINCOLN
DENVER
Arkansas R.
Lit. Colorado R.
SANTA FE
Albuquerque
PHOENIX
Tucson
AUSTIN
San Antonio
Rio Grande
Red R. of the North
Longitude
West
120
115
110
105
100
45
40
35
30
25

CANADA
LAKE SUPERIOR
MINNESOTA
WISCONSIN
MICHIGAN
IOWA
DES MOINES
ILLINOIS
INDIANA
OHIO
Cleveland
NEW YORK
Buffalo
PENNSYLVANIA
KENTUCKY
FRANKFORT
TENNESSEE
NASHVILLE
NORTH
CAROLINA
SOUTH
CAROLINA
Charleston
Savannah
GEORGIA
ATLANTA
ALABAMA
MISSISSIPPI
Mobile
LOUISIANA
BATON ROUGE
ARKANSAS
LITTLE ROCK
Memphis
MISSOURI
St. Louis
SPRINGFIELD
FLORIDA
Galveston
Montreal
OTTAWA
Portland
BOSTON
C. Hatteras
Wilmington
ATLANTIC OCEAN
GULF OF MEXICO
Greenwich
Dubuque
MADISON
Milwaukee
LANSING
Detroit
Chicago
Cincinnati
Wheeling
INDIANAPOLIS
RICHMOND
ALBANY

State. The number each State sends, depends upon its population.

The seat of government of a country is called the **capital**. **Washington** is the capital of the United States.

EXERCISE.— Who is now President? If a President dies in office, who succeeds him? How is the Vice President elected? (The people choose him.) When Queen Victoria dies, who will succeed her? (Her son *inherits* the office.) Where the chief ruler inherits his office, the government is a *monarchy*. England is a *monarchy*. The picture on p. 211 shows you a famous old building in Boston. It is called "The Cradle of American Liberty," on account of the spirited public meetings held there during the exciting times of the Revolutionary War.

XX.—REVIEW.

XVI. Where is the United States? How far does it extend? What regions compose the country? Where is the Atlantic Plain? The Appalachian system? The Central Plain? The table-land? What mountain systems border the table-land (p. 66)? What lies west of the Sierra system?

XVII. In what zone is the United States? Describe the climate. In what parts of the country is rain abundant? Which part is dry? Which is warmer, the Atlantic or the Pacific coast? Name some cultivated plants in the north, the middle, and the south.

XVIII. How many States in the Union? How many Territories? In which part are most of the States? The Territories? Where is the District of Columbia? Alaska? How did Alaska become ours?

XIX. What is the government of the United States? What is the population? What is a republic? What is the highest officer? By what body are the laws made? Of what does Congress consist? Of what is the Senate composed? The House? What is the capital of the United States? What is the capital of any country?

(MAP OF UNITED STATES.) What two oceans border upon the United States? What country at the north? What gulf and country at the south? What system of mountains in the eastern part? What two systems in the western part? Name the greatest river in the United States; its greatest two tributaries; two long rivers west of the Rocky Mountains; five great lakes north of the Ohio; a salt lake west of the Rocky Mountains.

Name the Territories. Which two border on Mexico? Name the States bordering upon the Atlantic; upon the Gulf of Mexico; upon the Pacific; upon the Mississippi; upon the Missouri; upon the Ohio; upon the Great Lakes. Which States do not border upon any of these waters? Name the **northernmost States of the Union**; the southernmost two States.

XXI.—NEW ENGLAND.
(PART I., PAGES 59-61.)

You have already learned much about this part of our country. A brave captain from England, who explored it when it was all a wilderness, called it *New England*, in honor of his own country across the Atlantic. The first white settlers are called "the Pilgrim Fathers." They were English people, and came over in a ship named "The Mayflower" in the year 1620. Their landing place was at *Plymouth*, on the coast of Massachusetts.

New England contains six States,—Maine, New Hampshire, Vermont, Massachusetts, Rhode Island, and Connecticut.

The **country** is rough, but beautiful. The river valleys and a part of the coast are the only level lands.

There are no very high **mountains**. The White Mountains, in New Hampshire, are the highest; and the Green Mountains, in Vermont, are the longest range.

The **lakes** are quite small, and the **rivers** are short and full of rapids and falls. Moosehead is the largest lake, and the Connecticut is the longest river.

A New England Homestead.

The **climate** is cool. The winters are long, but the summers are very pleasant.

EXERCISE. — (Open books to map of New England.) Find the States, mountains, river, and lake named in this lesson. Tell what surrounds Maine, beginning at the north. This is called bounding Maine. Bound each State. Find an island belonging to Maine; two islands belonging to Massachusetts.

XXII. — BUSINESS AND CITIES.

New England is not a great farming country; for the rough, stony land is hard to till, and many of the people prefer to get a living in some other way. Vermont is the only State where farming is the chief business. The others take advantage of their rapid streams for driving **mill wheels**, and their fine **harbors for** commerce. Besides these

BUSINESS AND CITIES. 217

occupations, Maine produces lumber, and builds ships, and Massachusetts sends many men to the fisheries. Vermont furnishes marble, and other States granite. Massachusetts and Rhode Island are more densely peopled than any other States in the Union.

The **leading occupations** in New England are manufacturing and commerce. Massachusetts, Rhode Island, and Connecticut manufacture most, and have the largest cities. Massachusetts has most commerce.

A Manufacturing Village.

Boston is the largest city in New England. It has about six hundred thousand inhabitants, and **is next** to New York in the extent of its commerce.

Providence, the second, is a large manufacturing city. *New Haven* is the seat of Yale College.

Lowell is famous for its cotton mills, and *Worcester* for its machinery. *Cambridge* contains Harvard University, the oldest college in New England.

EXERCISE. — (Open books to map of New England.) Which two States have the most seacoast? How do they make it useful? How does the map show the largest city in a State? (The name has a line drawn under it.) How is the capital of each state indicated? Find all the cities named in the lesson. Which of these are capitals? Find the other capital cities. Find a bay on the coast; a sound; two capes; four islands near the coast. Find two lakes; the five rivers which look the longest.

XXIII. — MAP LESSON.

NOTE. — To locate an *island*, tell its direction from the nearest coast; *mountains* or *lakes*, tell in what part, of what State, each is; *rivers*, tell where each rises, the course it takes, and the water into which it flows; *cities*, tell what and how situated each is. Thus: *Portland, the largest city of Maine, is situated in the southwestern part of the State, on the coast.*

Bound.	Locate.
MAINE.	Mount Desert Island, Moose'-head Lake, Pe-nob'-scot River, Ken-ne-bec' River, AU-GUS'-TA, Port'-land.
NEW HAMP'-SHIRE.	White Mountains, Mer'-ri-mac River, CON'-CORD, Man'-ches-ter.
VER-MONT'.	Green Mountains, Lake Champlain, MONT-PE'-LI-ER, Burlington.
MAS-SA-CHU'-SETTS.	Cape Cod, Cape Ann, Nan-tuck'-et, Marthas Vineyard, BOSTON, Lo'-well, Wor'-ces-ter (*Woos'-ter*), Cam'-bridge.
CONNECTICUT.	Long Island Sound, Con-nect'-i-cut River, HART'-FORD, New Haven.
RHODE ISLAND.	Nar-ra-gan'-sett Bay, PROV'-I-DENCE.

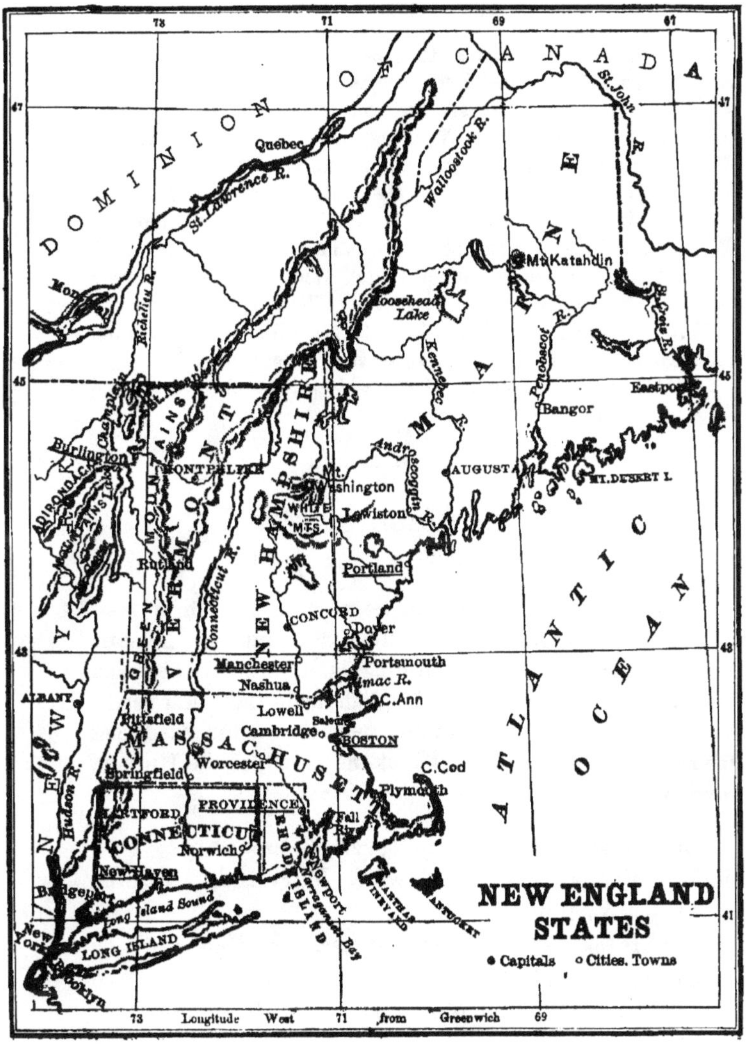
NEW ENGLAND STATES
• Capitals ○ Cities. Towns
DOMINION OF CANADA
Quebec
St. Lawrence R.
Walloostook R.
St. John R.
Mt. Katahdin
Moosehead Lake
Kennebec R.
Penobscot R.
St. Croix R.
Eastport
Bangor
MAINE
Androscoggin R.
AUGUSTA
MT. DESERT I.
Lewiston
Portland
Mt. Washington
WHITE MTS.
NEW HAMPSHIRE
CONCORD
Dover
Portsmouth
Manchester
Nashua
Merrimac R.
C. Ann
Lowell
Salem
Cambridge
BOSTON
C. Cod
Plymouth
Fall River
VERMONT
GREEN MOUNTAINS
MONTPELIER
Burlington
Champlain
Rutland
Connecticut R.
Richelieu R.
ADIRONDACK MTS.
NEW YORK
ALBANY
Hudson R.
Pittsfield
MASSACHUSETTS
Worcester
Springfield
HARTFORD
PROVIDENCE
CONNECTICUT
Norwich
RHODE ISLAND
Newport
Narragansett Bay
New Haven
Bridgeport
Long Island Sound
LONG ISLAND
New York
Brooklyn
MARTHAS VINEYARD
NANTUCKET
ATLANTIC OCEAN
73
71
69
67
47
45
43
41
Longitude West from Greenwich

XXIV.—REVIEW.

XXI. How many States in New England? Name them. When and where was the first settlement? What sort of country is New England? Where are the level lands? What and where are the highest mountains? What and where is the longest range? What is peculiar about the lakes and streams? Name the largest lake; the longest river. What is the climate of New England?

XXII. What are the leading occupations in New England? What else is done? What State makes farming most important? Which States lead in manufacturing? Which are most densely peopled? Which have the largest cities? What is the largest city in New England? The second in size? What is interesting about New Haven? Lowell? Worcester? Cambridge?

XXIII. Write the names of the States, mountains, rivers, and cities learned in Lesson XXIII.

XXV.—MIDDLE STATES.
(PART I., PAGES 37-47.)

These are the States which lie west and south of New England, in the Appalachian Mountains and the Atlantic Plain. They are rich in farming land, water power, and beds of coal and iron. The English made their first settlement this side of the Atlantic, near the mouth of James River, in 1607; and the Dutch at the mouth of the Hudson, seven years later.

The **Middle States** are seven,—New York, New Jersey, Pennsylvania, Delaware, Maryland, Virginia, and West Virginia.

Mountains extend from northeastern New York to southwestern Virginia. The Adirondacks are the highest; and the Alleghany range is the longest.

There are rich farming lands in the lower districts, while the mountain regions are mostly given up to forests, or used as pasturage for sheep and cattle.

The Hudson is the most important river.

Locks on the Erie Canal, at Lockport.

EXERCISE. — (Open books to map of Middle Atlantic States.) Find the States, mountains, and rivers named in this lesson. What rivers do you see, about which you have read? Find James River. Find Lake Ontario; Niagara River. What do you know (pp. 51, 52) about them? Who made the first settlement in New York, and where? The picture shows you some "locks" in the Erie Canal: what have you read about this canal? The locks enable boats to pass from one level in the bed of the canal to another.

XXVI. — BUSINESS AND CITIES.

(PART I., PAGES 12, 19, 37, 46, 62.)

This is a better farming region than New England; for there is more good land, and the climate is warmer. The four southern are chiefly farming States, raising grain, tobacco,

222　　GEOGRAPHICAL PRIMER.

and fruits. In the other three, manufacturing, mining, and commerce are also very important. Long Island and central New Jersey are hardly more than vast gardens for supplying the great cities with fruits and vegetables. The mountain forests employ many people in lumbering; and large numbers work at the oyster beds and other coast fisheries.

Agriculture, mining, manufacturing, and commerce are the leading **occupations.** Pennsylvania leads in mining, New York in manufacturing and commerce.

Newark, N.J.

The three northern States in this group, and the three southern in New England, constitute the leading **manufacturing and commercial region** in the United States.

Many of the **greatest cities** of the Union are in the Middle States. **New York,** the largest city in the western hemisphere, contains about three and a half millions of people. Its commerce extends to all important countries, and it has a great amount of other business.

Manhattan is its chief borough.

The borough of *Brooklyn*, on Long Island is opposite Manhattan.

Philadelphia is famous for manufacturing. It has more than a million of people.

Baltimore is a great market for tobacco and grain.

The other large cities are Pittsburg, Buffalo, **Washington,** Newark, and Jersey City. But there are many fine cities of smaller size.

EXERCISE.—(Open books to map of Middle States.) What great water route (p. 46) crosses New York? Where does it reach the coast? What cities are there for the gardens of Long Island and New Jersey to supply? Find each of the great cities named in this lesson. What have you read about the first three? About the next three? On the opposite page you see a part of Newark, with its smoking factory chimneys. Like Pittsburg, it is a famous place for manufacturing. Jersey City is situated like Brooklyn, with only a river separating it from the borough of Manhattan. Find the capital of each State; of the United States.

XXVII.—REVIEW.

XXV. Name the Middle States. When and where were the first settlements in these States? What part of this region is mountainous? Name the highest mountains; the principal range. Where are the good farming lands? Name the most important rivers. What large river begins in Pennsylvania? What State has most lakes? Describe the climate.

XXVI. What are the chief occupations? Which are mostly farming States? What do they raise? What States form the greatest manufacturing and commercial region in the country? What State leads in these occupations? In mining? What great cities are there in these States? Which one is largest? What have you learned about New York? About Philadelphia? Baltimore? Name the other large cities in these States.

XXVIII.—MAP LESSON.

Bound.	Locate.
NEW YORK.	Long Island, Adirondack Mountains, Catskill Mountains, Hudson River, ALBANY, New York, Buffalo.
NEW JERSEY.	Cape May, Delaware River, TRENTON, Newark, Jersey City.
PENN-SYL-VA'-NI-A.	Alleghany Mountains, Blue Ridge, Susquehanna River, Ohio River, HARRISBURG, Philadelphia, Pittsburg.
DELAWARE.	Delaware Bay, DO'-VER, Wilmington.
MA'-RY-LAND.	Chesapeake Bay, Po-to'-mac River, AN-NAP'-O-LIS, Baltimore.
VIR-GIN'-I-A.	Blue Ridge Mountains, James River, RICH'-MOND.
WEST VIRGINIA.	Alleghany Mountains, CHARLESTON, Wheel'-ing.
DIST. CO-LUM'-BI-A.	WASHINGTON.

How would you go by water from Albany to Philadelphia? From Philadelphia to Baltimore? From Baltimore to Washington? From New York to Richmond? From Buffalo to New York? Write the names of all States, mountains, rivers, and cities learned in Lesson XXVIII.

XXIX.—SOUTHERN STATES.
(PART I., PAGES 33–37.)

In the journey down the Mississippi we saw cotton growing soon after passing the mouth of the Ohio. All the States lying farther south than this, whether in the Atlantic Plain or in the Central Plain, produce cotton, and most of them make it their principal crop: hence all of them together are sometimes called the *cotton States.* Four border on the Atlantic, four on the Gulf, and two are inland. Those on the coast are often called the *South Atlantic States* and *Gulf States.*

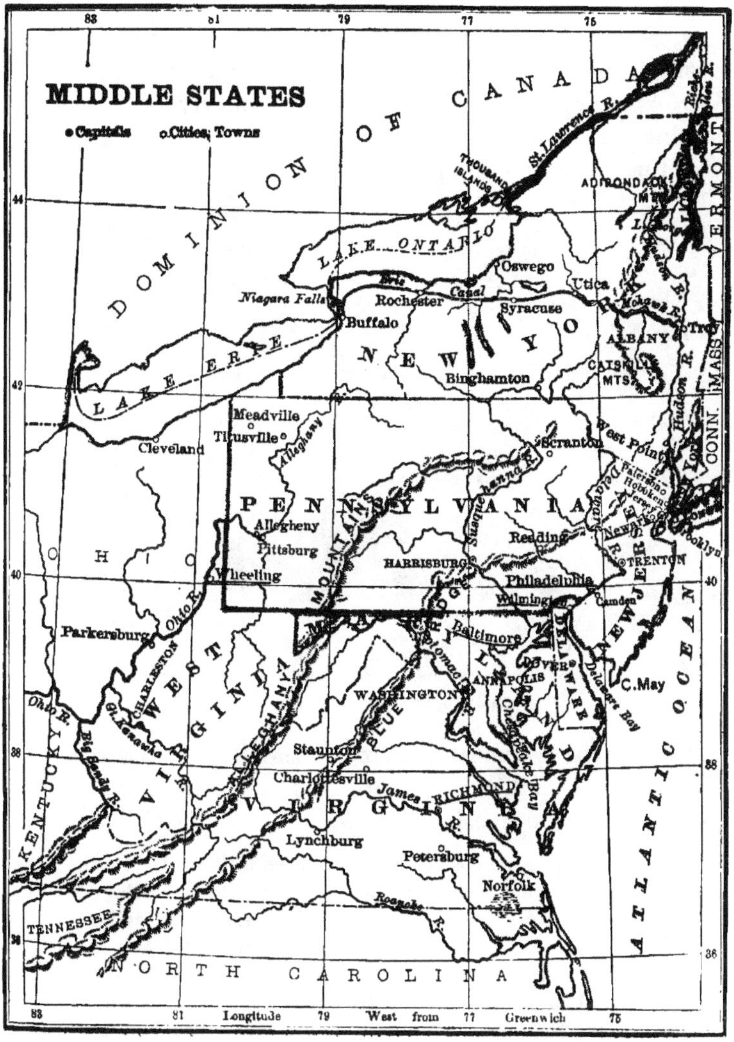
MIDDLE STATES
• Capitals
o Cities; Towns
DOMINION OF CANADA
St. Lawrence R.
THOUSAND ISLANDS
ADIRONDACK MTS.
VERMONT
LAKE ONTARIO
LAKE ERIE
Niagara Falls
Buffalo
Rochester
Erie Canal
Oswego
Syracuse
Utica
Mohawk R.
ALBANY
Troy
NEW YORK
Binghamton
CATSKILL MTS.
Hudson R.
MASS.
CONN.
West Point
Scranton
Meadville
Titusville
Cleveland
Allegheny
PENNSYLVANIA
Allegheny
Pittsburg
Wheeling
Susquehanna R.
Reading
HARRISBURG
Philadelphia
Wilmington
Camden
TRENTON
Paterson
Hoboken
Jersey City
Newark
Brooklyn
NEW JERSEY
Delaware R.
OHIO
Ohio R.
Parkersburg
CHARLESTON
WEST VIRGINIA
MOUNTAINS
Baltimore
ANNAPOLIS
DOVER
DELAWARE
MARYLAND
Delaware Bay
C. May
WASHINGTON
Potomac R.
Chesapeake Bay
BLUE RIDGE
ALLEGHANY
Gt. Kanawha
Big Sandy R.
KENTUCKY
Staunton
Charlottesville
James R.
RICHMOND
VIRGINIA
Lynchburg
Petersburg
Norfolk
Roanoke R.
TENNESSEE
NORTH CAROLINA
ATLANTIC OCEAN
83
81
79
77
75
44
42
40
38
36
Longitude West from Greenwich

There are ten **cotton-growing States,** — North Carolina, South Carolina, Georgia, Florida, Alabama, Mississippi, Louisiana, Texas, Tennessee, and Arkansas [*Ar'-kan-saw*]. The **surface** consists mostly of very productive plains. The Black Mountains in North Carolina are the loftiest part of the Appalachian system.

Square in San Antonio, Tex.

This is the **warmest** portion of the United States. The winter is mild everywhere, and the southernmost parts rarely have freezing weather.

EXERCISE. — (Open books to map of Southern States.) Which is not shown on this map? Find it on the map of the United States. Which States extend farthest south? Which lie farthest north? Find the States, mountains, and rivers named in this lesson. Why is this the warmest part of the United States? Bound each State, and name its capital. The picture shows a small part of San Antonio, in Texas. It is one of the oldest towns in **America.**

XXX.—BUSINESS AND CITIES.
(Part I., Pages 9, 10, 35, 36.)

Ever since these States were settled, agriculture has been their main business,—until recently almost the only one. This is not strange, because the level surface and rich soil make cultivation easy and crops abundant; and the market, too, is sure, for the climate favors the growth of things needed for use where they cannot be produced. But the Southern States have stores of coal and iron and abundant water power, which are now used in manufacturing, especially in Georgia. A few cities owe their growth to their manufactures, but most depend on the cotton trade for business.

Agriculture is the **main business** of these States. Besides the great cotton crop, rice grows on lowlands

New Orleans, La.

along the coast, and the warmest portions produce sugar and tropical fruits.

Manufacturing increases rapidly. Iron and cotton manufactures take the lead.

New Orleans is the only **great city**. It is the main center of the Mississippi trade, and the largest cotton market in the world.

Charleston, Savannah, Mobile, Galveston, and Memphis are **cotton markets**. Atlanta and Birmingham have extensive iron works, and Augusta has cotton mills.

EXERCISE. — (Open books to map of Southern States.) In what part of our country can these States sell their cotton? Why is not cotton raised in New England? The coal and iron come mainly from the mountains. Which States would you suppose have the most water power? Why? Find the cotton markets named in the lesson; the manufacturing cities; the largest city in each State. (Dallas is the largest in Texas.) What have you read about New Orleans? Find the capital of each State. The cotton States have not very many good harbors for large vessels.

XXXI. — MAP LESSON.

Bound. **Locate.**

N. CAR-O-LI'-NA. Cape Hat'-te-ras, Blue Ridge, Black Mountains, RA'-LEIGH (Raw'-), Wil'-ming-ton.

S. CAROLINA. San-tee' River, CO-LUM'-BI-A, Charleston.

GEOR'-GI-A. Altamaha (Aωl-ta-ma-haw') River, Blue Ridge, AT-LAN'-TA, Augusta, Sa-van'-nah.

FLOR'-I-DA. Cape Sable, Ap-a-lach-i-co'-la River, Lake O-ke-cho'-bee, TAL-LA-HAS'-SEE, Jacksonville.

AL-A-BA'-MA. Alabama River, MONT-GOM'-E-RY (-gum'-), Mo-bile' (beel').

MISSISSIPPI. Mississippi River, JACKSON, Vicks'-burg.

LOU-I-SI-A'-NA. Red River, BATON ROUGE (Bat'-un Roozh'), New Orleans.

TEN-NES-SEE'. Tennessee River, NASHVILLE, Mem'-phis.

AR'-KAN-SAS. Arkansas River, LITTLE ROCK.

TEX'-AS. (Map of United States.) Rio Grande River, AUSTIN, Dallas, Gal'-ves-ton, San Antonio.

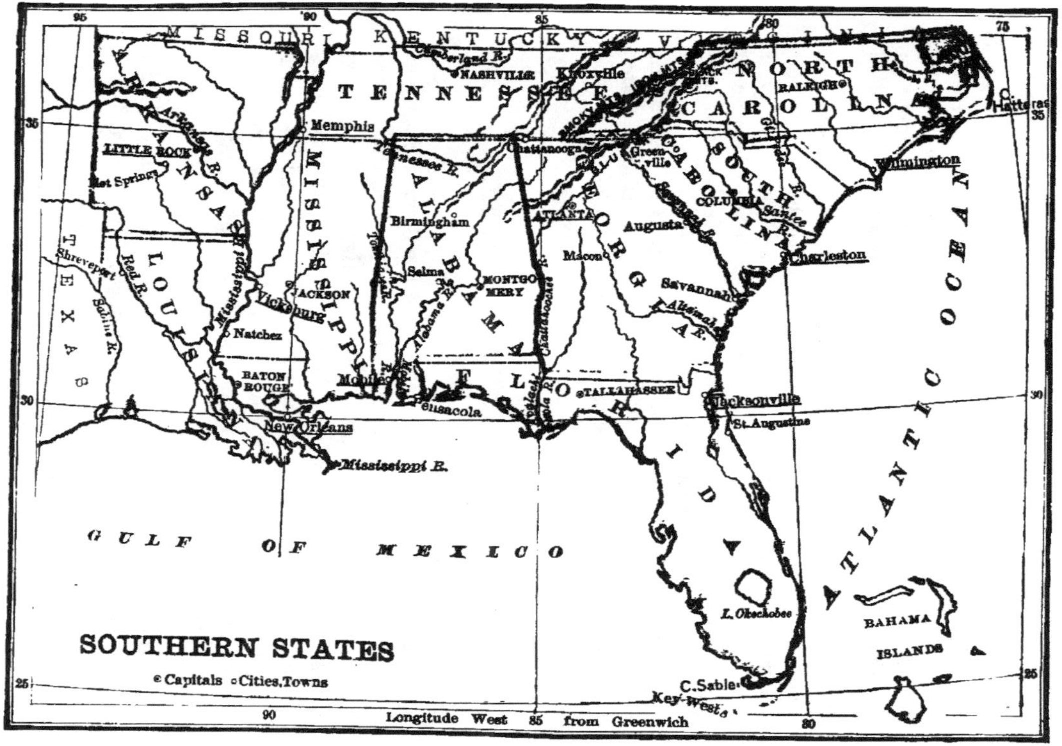
SOUTHERN STATES
Capitals
Cities, Towns
Longitude West from Greenwich
MISSOURI
KENTUCKY
TENNESSEE
NORTH CAROLINA
SOUTH CAROLINA
GEORGIA
ALABAMA
MISSISSIPPI
ARKANSAS
LOUISIANA
TEXAS
FLORIDA
GULF OF MEXICO
ATLANTIC OCEAN
BAHAMA ISLANDS
NASHVILLE
Knoxville
Memphis
Chattanooga
LITTLE ROCK
Hot Springs
Birmingham
ATLANTA
Augusta
Macon
Savannah
Charleston
COLUMBIA
Greenville
RALEIGH
Wilmington
Selma
MONTGOMERY
JACKSON
Vicksburg
Natchez
BATON ROUGE
New Orleans
Mobile
Pensacola
TALLAHASSEE
Jacksonville
St. Augustine
Shreveport
L. Okechobee
C. Sable
Key West
C. Hatteras
Cumberland R.
Tennessee R.
Arkansas R.
Red R.
Sabine R.
Mississippi R.
Alabama R.
Tombigbee R.
Chattahoochee R.
Altamaha R.
Savannah R.
Santee R.
Apalachicola R.
95
90
85
80
75
35
30
25

XXXII.—REVIEW.

XXIX. Name the Southern States. What is their general surface? What mountains in this region? Name the principal range; the highest part of the Appalachian system. How high are the Black Mountains? What great river crosses the cotton States? Describe the climate.

XXX. What is the main occupation of these States? The chief crop? What else is raised? What other business is now important? What kinds of manufactures? How many great cities in the cotton States? How is New Orleans important? What is the business of the other cities? Name the cotton markets; the manufacturing cities.

Write about the country in the southern parts of the Atlantic and Central Plains (pp. 9, 35, 36). Write the names of all States, rivers, mountains, and cities learned in Lesson XXXI.

XXXIII.—CENTRAL STATES.
(Part I., Pages 29-32, 47-50.)

The middle and northern portion of the Central Plain contains fourteen States, which together are called the *Central States*. Three of the States are in the higher prairie region west and southwest of the Missouri. The Central States have access to the Gulf by the Mississippi and its tributaries; and to the Atlantic by the Great Lakes, the Erie Canal, and the Hudson, or by the Great Lakes and the St. Lawrence.

The **Central States** are fourteen,—Kentucky, Ohio, Indiana, Illinois, Michigan, Wisconsin, Minnesota, Iowa, Missouri, Kansas, Nebraska, North Dakota, South Dakota, and Oklahoma (see map of United States).

The **surface** consists principally of very fertile plains,

CENTRAL STATES. 231

partly rolling and partly flat. West of the Mississippi most of the country is prairie land.

The Mississippi **river,** the Missouri, and the Ohio flow through the Central States, making a navigable water course of great value. The **Great Lakes** border these States, and Minnesota has many small lakes.

At the extreme **north** the summer is rather short, but hot; the winter long and cold. At the **south** the summer is much longer, and the winter is mild.

Chicago Stock Yard.

EXERCISE. — (Open books to map of Central States.) Which States are shown here? Which great lakes? Which great lake is wholly in the Central States? In what State is most of Lake Michigan? What other States border on it? What States border on Lake Superior? Huron? Erie? Mississippi River? Ohio River? What river do you see on the western boundary of Minnesota? Where (map of North America) does this stream reach the sea? A lake feeding the Minnesota almost touches one feeding the Red River; where do its waters reach the sea? Find Minnesota River; Illinois; Cumberland; Des Moines. Bound each State (map of the United States for North Dakota, South Dakota, Nebraska, Kansas, and Oklahoma). Find their capitals. Locate **Chicago,** St. Louis, Cleveland, Cincinnati, Detroit, and Milwaukee.

XXXIV.—BUSINESS AND CITIES.
(Part I., Pages 22, 33, 48.)

The Central States might be called the grain farm and pasture of the Union; for grain growing and stock raising are as important here as cotton planting farther south. The surface and soil are as good here as there; but the crops are different on account of the climate. This region has in-

A Grain Elevator.

creased very rapidly in population and wealth, and has large, rich cities. West of the Mississippi there are not so many people as there are farther east; but many thousands are going there every year.

Agriculture is the **main business** of the Central

States. **Wheat and** corn are the great crops; but tobacco is important in Kentucky and Missouri.

Great numbers of horses, cattle, sheep, and swine are also raised here.

Manufacturing is fast increasing. It consists mostly of flouring, curing and packing meat, and making tools and machinery for farming.

Copper is **mined** on the southern shore of Lake Superior, and iron, lead, and coal in several places.

The **greatest cities** are Chicago, St. Louis, Cincinnati, and Cleveland. Next come Milwaukee, Detroit, Minneapolis, Louisville, Omaha, St. Paul, Kansas City, and Indianapolis.

EXERCISE.— (Open books to map of Central States.) Find each of the cities named in the lesson. Which are on the Lakes? On the Mississippi? On the Ohio? What do you know about Chicago? St. Louis? Cincinnati? What tobacco States (p. 222) have you learned of farther east? Which (p. 209) grows farther north—wheat, or corn? Find the capital of each State; the largest city in each. What do you know (p. 29) about Minneapolis and St. Paul. There are rapids at Louisville, but boats go up the Ohio all the way to Pittsburg: how do you suppose they get past the rapids? (By a canal.)

XXXV.—REVIEW

XXXIII. Name the Central States. What part of the Central Plain is mostly prairie land? What great streams and lakes in this region? Which great lake is wholly in the Central States? Describe the climate. Where are the Cumberland Mountains? Ozark Mountains? Black Hills?

XXXIV. What is the great business of the Central States? The leading crops? Which States produce tobacco? What tobacco States have you learned of farther east? Which grows farther north — wheat, or corn? What manufacturing is done in the Central States? What mining? What great cities in the Central States? What do you know about Chicago? St. Louis? Cleveland? Cincinnati? Which cities are next them in size?

XXXVI.— MAP LESSON.

Bound.	Locate.
KENTUCKY.	Cum'-ber-land River, FRANK'-FORT, Lou'-is-ville.
OHIO.	Ohio River, Co-LUM'-BUS, Cincinnati, Cleve'-land.
INDIANA.	Wabash River, IN-DI-AN-AP'-O-LIS.
ILLINOIS.	Illinois River, SPRINGFIELD, Chicago.
MICHIGAN.	Lake Michigan, Mackinac Strait, LANSING, Detroit.
WISCONSIN.	Wisconsin River, MAD'-I-SON, Mil-wau'-kee.
MINNESOTA.	Itasca Lake, Mississippi River, ST. PAUL, Minneapolis.
IOWA.	Des Moines River (*De Moin'*), DES MOINES (city).
MISSOURI.	Mis-sou'-ri River, JEFFERSON CITY, St. Louis.
KANSAS.	TO-PE'-KA, Kansas City, Wich'-i-ta, Leav'-en-worth.
NEBRASKA.	Platte River, LINCOLN, O'-ma-ha.
NORTH DAKOTA.	BISMARCK, Fargo.
SOUTH DAKOTA.	Black Hills, PIERRE, Sioux Falls.
OKLAHOMA.	(Map of United States.) GUTHRIE.

Write the names of all the States, lakes, rivers, and cities learned in Lesson XXXVI.

XXXVII.— THE PACIFIC STATES.
(PART I., PAGES 65–70.)

In some respects, this is the most remarkable portion of the United States. The highest two mountain systems are here; the only great table-land is between them; and the only part of the country which does not naturally produce useful plants is on the table-land. Here, too, are smoking volcanoes, spouting geysers, and cañons so narrow and deep that the streams at the bottom of them cannot be used even for moistening the soil.

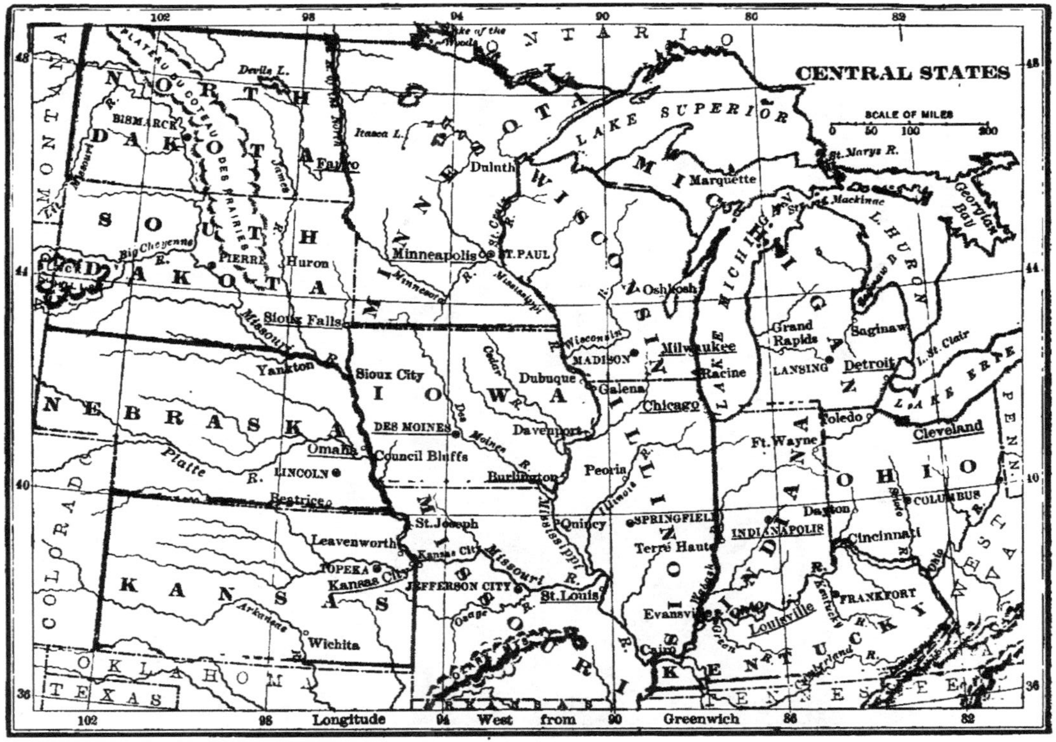
CENTRAL STATES
SCALE OF MILES
0 50 100 200
NORTH DAKOTA
SOUTH DAKOTA
NEBRASKA
KANSAS
MINNESOTA
IOWA
MISSOURI
WISCONSIN
ILLINOIS
MICHIGAN
INDIANA
OHIO
KENTUCKY
MONTANA
COLORADO
OKLAHOMA
TEXAS
ARKANSAS
TENNESSEE
WEST VA.
PENN.
ONTARIO
LAKE SUPERIOR
LAKE MICHIGAN
L. HURON
LAKE ERIE
Georgian Bay
L. St. Clair
BISMARCK
Fargo
PIERRE
Huron
Sioux Falls
Yankton
Sioux City
Omaha
Council Bluffs
LINCOLN
Beatrice
Leavenworth
TOPEKA
Kansas City
Wichita
Minneapolis
ST. PAUL
Duluth
DES MOINES
Dubuque
Davenport
Burlington
St. Joseph
JEFFERSON CITY
St. Louis
Quincy
Peoria
SPRINGFIELD
Galena
Chicago
Cairo
MADISON
Oshkosh
Milwaukee
Racine
Marquette
Grand Rapids
LANSING
Saginaw
Detroit
Toledo
Ft. Wayne
INDIANAPOLIS
Terre Haute
Evansville
Dayton
Cincinnati
COLUMBUS
Cleveland
Louisville
FRANKFORT
Devils L.
Itasca L.
PLATEAU DU COTEAU DES PRAIRIES
Missouri R.
James R.
Big Cheyenne R.
Platte R.
Arkansas
Minnesota R.
Mississippi R.
Des Moines R.
Cedar R.
Wisconsin R.
Illinois R.
Wabash R.
Ohio R.
Osage R.
Kentucky R.
Cumberland R.
Green R.
Scioto R.
St. Marys R.
Mackinac
102 98 94 90 86 82
48 44 40 36
Longitude West from Greenwich

This group contains nine **States** and two **Territories.**
The States are: Montana, Wyoming, and Colorado, crossed by the Rocky Mountains; Idaho, Utah, and Nevada, lying on the great table-land; Washington, Oregon, and California, upon the Pacific coast. The Territories are Arizona and New Mexico, on the table-land.

On the **table-land,** excepting in Idaho, the country is so dry that not much of the surface is fit for agriculture, except where it can be irrigated.

The **Rocky Mountain States** are all rich in silver and gold, and Montana has very productive copper mines. Colorado, in 1895, produced more gold than any other State in the Union; and the United States, more than any other country in the world.

An Indian Papoose.

The **Pacific States** have the broadest and most fertile valleys in the high western half of the United States. California was once the greatest gold State; but much has since been discovered in Colorado and elsewhere.

EXERCISE.—(Open books to map of Pacific States.) Find each State and Territory named in the map. Which are crossed by the Rocky Mountains? Which by the Sierra Nevada and Cascade Mountains? Bound each State; each Territory. **Find** Missouri River; Yellowstone; Colorado; Columbia; Great Salt Lake. **Find** Yellowstone Park. Write about the table-land.

XXXVIII.—BUSINESS AND CITIES.
(PART I., PAGES 70-74.)

A large part of this vast region is unfit, by nature, for many kinds of business. But even the dry table-land is productive where the surface can be *irrigated*. This is done by leading water from some stream, through artificial channels, and distributing it over the ground where it is needed. Much fine farming land has been thus made.

California Fruit Ranch.

The three States bordering on the **Pacific** are more uniformly settled than the others in this extensive division. Elsewhere there are few people except in the mining districts and along the lines of the railroad.

In **Montana, Idaho,** and the States on the Pacific, immense areas are given to cattle raising, wool growing, and wheat farming. **Washington** and **Oregon** have vast forests and excellent fisheries.

California, besides wheat farms, has large districts devoted to orchards and vineyards. Great quantities of fruit are shipped to eastern markets. San Francisco, in California, is the chief city.

Others are *Sacramento*, the capital of California; *Portland*, in Oregon; *Tacoma* and *Seattle*, in Washington; *Salt Lake City*, in the irrigated lands of Utah; and *Denver*, in Colorado, the center of business for the mining region.

EXERCISE. — (Open books to map of Pacific States.) Find San Francisco. Find the largest city in each State; the capital of each. Find Salt Lake City. Write about the discovery of gold. (Page 72.)

XXXIX. — MAP LESSON.

Bound.	Locate.
MONTANA.	Yellowstone River, Missouri River, HELENA, Butte.
WYOMING.	Yellowstone Park, Black Hills, CHEYENNE'.
COLORADO.	Rocky Mountains, DENVER, Pueblo.
NEW MEXICO.	Rio Grande, SANTA FÉ, Albuquerque.
IDAHO.	BOISE.
UTAH.	Wasatch Mountains, SALT LAKE CITY.
ARIZONA.	PHŒNIX, Tucson.
NEVADA.	Colorado River, CARSON CITY, Virginia City, Reno.
WASHINGTON.	Cape Flattery, OLYMPIA, Seattle.
OREGON.	Cascade Mountains, Columbia River, SALEM, Portland.
CALIFORNIA.	Sierra Nevada Mountains, SACRAMENTO, San Francisco.

XL. — REVIEW.

XXXVII. Name the Pacific States and Territories. What kind of surface has this region? What large barren district? What is the highest land in the United States? How high is Mount Whitney? What is peculiar about the lakes and streams in this region? Describe the climate.

XXXVIII. What parts of this region have most people? Where are gold and silver found? What pursuits are important in California? in Oregon? What can you say about San Francisco? Denver? Salt Lake City? Name the capital and largest city of each State.

XXXIX. Write the names of the States, Territories, mountains, rivers, and cities learned in Lesson XXXIX.

PACIFIC STATES
AND
TERRITORIES
SCALE OF MILES
0 50 100 200
DOMINION OF CANADA
WASHINGTON
OREGON
IDAHO
MONTANA
WYOMING
NEVADA
UTAH
COLORADO
CALIFORNIA
ARIZONA
NEW MEXICO
NORTH DAKOTA
SOUTH DAKOTA
NEBRASKA
PACIFIC OCEAN
MEXICO
Spokane
Walla Walla
Mt. Rainier
Mt. Hood
Mt. Baker
Ft. Benton
Missouri
HELENA
Butte
Virginia City
BOISE
Union Pass
Fremont Peak
CHEYENNE
Great Salt Lake
Ogden
SALT LAKE CITY
Virginia City
CARSON CITY
DENVER
Leadville
Pikes Peak
Pueblo
Stockton
Mt. Shasta
Mt. Whitney
Pt. Concepcion
Los Angeles
San Diego
Colorado
PHOENIX
Tucson
SANTA FE
Las Vegas
Albuquerque
Grande
G. of California
118 Longitude 114 West from 110 Greenwich 106

XLI.—COLD COUNTRIES OF NORTH AMERICA.

(Part I., Pages 52-56, 78-82.)

We have learned that the greater part of this continent, north of the United States, is a cold forest land with few

Montreal.

inhabitants but Indians, and that the Arctic shores, where the Eskimos live, are colder and almost barren. In the sea to the northeast, are Greenland and Iceland, which belong to Denmark. All of the northern part of the continent, except Alaska, belongs to Great Britain. It is divided into several provinces, which together form the *Dominion of Canada*. Montreal is the only great city of the Dominion, but Quebec is older.

Newfoundland also belongs to Great Britain. It is not a part of the Dominion of Canada, but has a separate government.

EXERCISE. — (Open books to map of North America.) Find Greenland; Iceland; Alaska. To what countries do they belong? Find the Dominion of Canada. Find three great rivers in it; three large lakes. You remember Red River on the western boundary of Minnesota (see map, p. 235); into what lake does it flow? Find Montreal; Quebec. Write what you know (pp. 53, 54) about them.

XLII.—THE WARM, SOUTHERN COUNTRIES.
(PART I., PAGES 82-88.)

We know that the countries of North America at the south of us are as much warmer than ours, as those north of us are colder. We remember the hot coast lands, with their abundance of interesting and valuable plants; and the gradual change as the land rises, until in the high, cool interior, the fields and forests look almost like our own. We have read, too, of terrific volcanoes in these countries, and of earthquakes that shake down people's houses.

South of the United States, are the hot countries of *Mexico*, *Central America*, and the *West Indies*.

Mexico is a republic, made up of many small States, united under one government. *Mexico*, its capital, is on a high table-land in the interior.

Central America consists of six small, independent republics, and a British colony. A great ship canal is being constructed across the Isthmus of Panama to connect the Atlantic and Pacific oceans.

The **West Indies** include four large islands, and a great number of very small ones. *Cuba* and *Haiti* are much the largest. The island of Cuba is famous for its sugar cane and tobacco. *Havana* is the capital and largest city *Porto Rico* belongs to the United States.

EXERCISE. — (Open books to map of North America.) Find Mexico; Central America; Cuba; Haiti. What line passes just north of Cuba? In what zone are these hot countries? In what zone is the northern part of Mexico? Do you suppose this part to be cooler, or warmer, than the southern? Why? What small islands of the West Indies lie north of the tropic? The little one farthest east was the first land found by Columbus. Its name is *Salvador.*

XLIII.—MAP LESSON.

Bound.		Locate.
NORTH AMERICA.	Greenland.	Montreal.
DOMINION OF CANADA.	Iceland.	OT'-TA-WA.
UNITED STATES.	Ja-mai'-ca (-ma'-).	WASHINGTON.
MEXICO.	Hudson Bay.	Chicago.
CENTRAL AMERICA.	Gulf of Mexico.	Philadelphia.
A-LAS'-KA.	Gulf of St. Lawrence.	New York.
NEW'-FOUND-LAND.	Gulf of California.	San Francisco.
CUBA.	Car-ib-be'-an Sea.	MEXICO (city).
HAI'-TI.	Pan-a-ma' Isthmus.	HA-VAN'-A.

XLIV.—REVIEW.

XLI. What is Danish America? To what country does the northern part of North America belong? What part of the Dominion of Canada is peopled by civilized men? How is it divided? What island forms a separate province? How is the Dominion governed? What is the capital? Name the other chief cities.

XLII. What countries lie south of the United States? What is Mexico? What and where is its capital? Of what does Central America consist? What do the West Indies include? Name the largest two islands? What is interesting about Cuba? **What is its chief city?** To what country does Porto Rico belong?

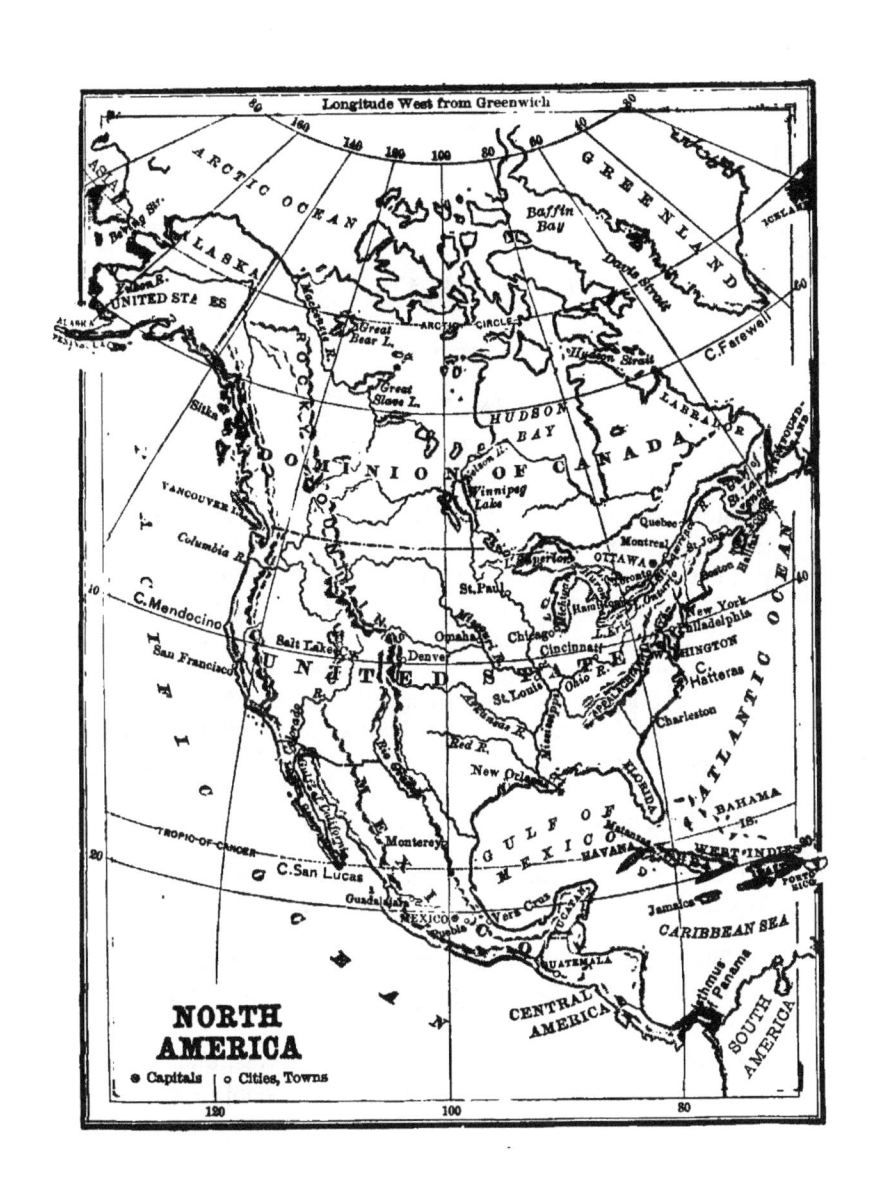

NORTH AMERICA

SOUTH AMERICA.

XLV.—COUNTRIES OF THE PLAINS.
(PART I., PAGES 89-96, 102-107.)

SOUTH AMERICA is a remarkable continent. It has the highest mountains on the globe excepting the Himalaya, the most extensive forests in the world, and vast treeless plains that at one season are covered with the richest vegetation, and at another are parched by the sun and swept by flames until they seem like a desert. It lies mainly in the Torrid Zone; yet even here the valleys between the Andes have the temperature of spring, and the tops bear snow throughout the year. All the countries of South America are republics, excepting Guiana, which is a small mountain land, belonging to countries in Europe.

The hard names in this lesson are pronounced thus:—

Bra-zil', Ven-e-zwee'-la, Pah-rah-gwi', Oo-roo-gwi', Ar-jen-tc'-na, Re'-o de Zha-na'-e-ro, Bo'-nus A'-riz, Gee-ah'-na.

The **plains** of South America contain five countries,— Brazil, Venezuela, Paraguay, Uruguay, and Argentina.

Brazil includes the larger part of the silvas, and has valuable gold districts. There are few people except in the coast regions.

Agriculture is the **chief pursuit**, and coffee the prin-

COUNTRIES OF THE PLAINS. 245

cipal crop. *Rio de Janeiro*, the capital, is the greatest coffee market in the world. *Bahia* is also a large city.

Venezuela, Argentina, Paraguay, and **Uruguay** contain the vast llanos, pampas, and other treeless plains.

Cattle raising is the **main business,** with agriculture in some of the best districts.

Buenos Ayres, and *Montevideo*, on the La Plata, are the only large cities in these four countries. They are famous markets for hides, horns, and tallow.

Plaza, Buenos Ayres.

EXERCISE. — (Open books to map of South America.) Find Guiana. What is it? Bound each of the countries of the plains. Find their capitals. Which of these countries is the largest? Which are in the Torrid Zone? In what zone are the others? Which part of these temperate countries is warmest? Why? On the Amazon where do you see the sun at noon? In our country, where? In Uruguay, where? Why? (One must always look toward the Torrid Zone to see the sun at noon.) What (p. 95) are the silvas? What (p. 102) are the llanos? What (p. 105) are the pampas?

XLVI.—COUNTRIES OF THE ANDES.
(Part L., Pages 97–101.)

You remember that the Andes extend along the whole western coast of South America, shutting off from the Pacific all the rich plains. You know that the larger part is a great double range, with a long, high, wide valley between the

A Scene in Ecuador, S.A.

tops. The mountains are highest, and the tops of the two ridges widest apart, in the middle portion, where the inner valley contains a large lake. Here, in the eastern ridge, are peaks which are nearly five miles high. **The hard names** of this lesson are pronounced on p. 248.

The **countries of the Andes** are Colombia, Ecuador, Peru, Bolivia, and Chile. All but Chile extend across the mountains into the silvas. All are torrid except Chile, which has a climate similar to our own.

These countries all have rich deposits of gold, silver, and copper; but Chile is the only one which attends much to **mining**.

In the four torrid countries most of the **people live** in the valleys among the Andes, which have a better climate than the lowlands.

Santiago, the capital of Chile, *Valparaiso* also in Chile, and *Lima*, the capital of Peru, are the **largest cities** on the west side of the Andes.

EXERCISE. — (Open books to map of South America.) Name the countries of the Andes; their capitals. Do these cities seem to be among the mountains, or in the lowlands? Why do people prefer to live in the highlands? Where do you see lakes in the wide valley? The highest mountains lie east of that largest lake; what capital is near them?

XLVII.—REVIEW.

XLV. Name the countries of the plains. What is the chief pursuit in Brazil? The principal crop? What minerals has Brazil? What part is most peopled? What great cities has Brazil? What do you know about Rio de Janeiro? What is the chief business of the other countries of the plains? What are the largest cities of these four countries?

XLVI. What countries are crossed by the Andes? Which one is on the west side? What is the climate of these countries? What valuable minerals have they? In which one is most attention given to mining? What is the best part of the torrid countries to live in? Why? What are the two greatest cities on the Pacific side of the mountains? Where and how high are the eastern Andes?

XLVIII.—MAP LESSON.

Bound.	Locate.	
GUI-A′-NA.	Cape Horn.	Buenos Ayres.
VEN-E-ZUE′-LA.	Ti-er′-ra del Fu-e′-go.	San-ti-a′-go (-*ah*′-).
BRA-ZIL′.	Andes Mountains.	Li′-ma.
PA-RA-GUAY′.	Am′-a-zon River.	La Paz (*Lah*).
U-RU-GUAY′.	Pa-ra-na′ River (-*nah*′).	Qui′-to (*Ke*′-).
AR-GEN-TI′-NA.	La Pla′-ta River.	George′-town.
CHI′-LE.	Orinoco River.	Par-a-mar′-i-bo.
BO-LIV′-I-A.	Ca-ra′-cas (-*rah*′-).	Ca-yenne′.
PE-RU′.	Rio de Janeiro.	Bo-go-ta′ (-*tah*′).
EC-UA-DOR′ (-*wa*-).	A-sun′-ci-on.	Val-pa-rai′-so (-*ri*′-).
CO-LOM′-BI-A.	Mon-te-vid′-e-o.	Ba-hi′-a (-*e*′-).

XLIX.—WESTERN HEMISPHERE (Examination).

What two continents in the western hemisphere? How are they connected? In what zone is most of North America? Most of South America? What part of North America is in the Torrid Zone? What part of South America is in the Temperate Zone? Name the countries of North America; of South America. What parts of each continent belong to European governments? Which is the most important country of North America? Of South America? What is the government of the United States? Of Brazil? Of all the other independent countries of the New World?

Of what does the United States consist? Name the States; the Territories; the capital. In what part of the United States are manufacturing and commerce most important? In what parts is agriculture the great business? What is the chief crop of the Southern States? Of the Central? Where are coal and iron mined? Gold and silver? Copper? Name the great cities of the United States,—naming, in New England, *one*; in the Middle States, *three*; in the Southern States, *one*; in the Central States, *three*; in the Pacific States, *one*.

Name the largest city in the **Dominion** of Canada; in Mexico; in the West Indies. Name the largest cities of South America,— on the eastern coast, *three*; on the western, *two*.

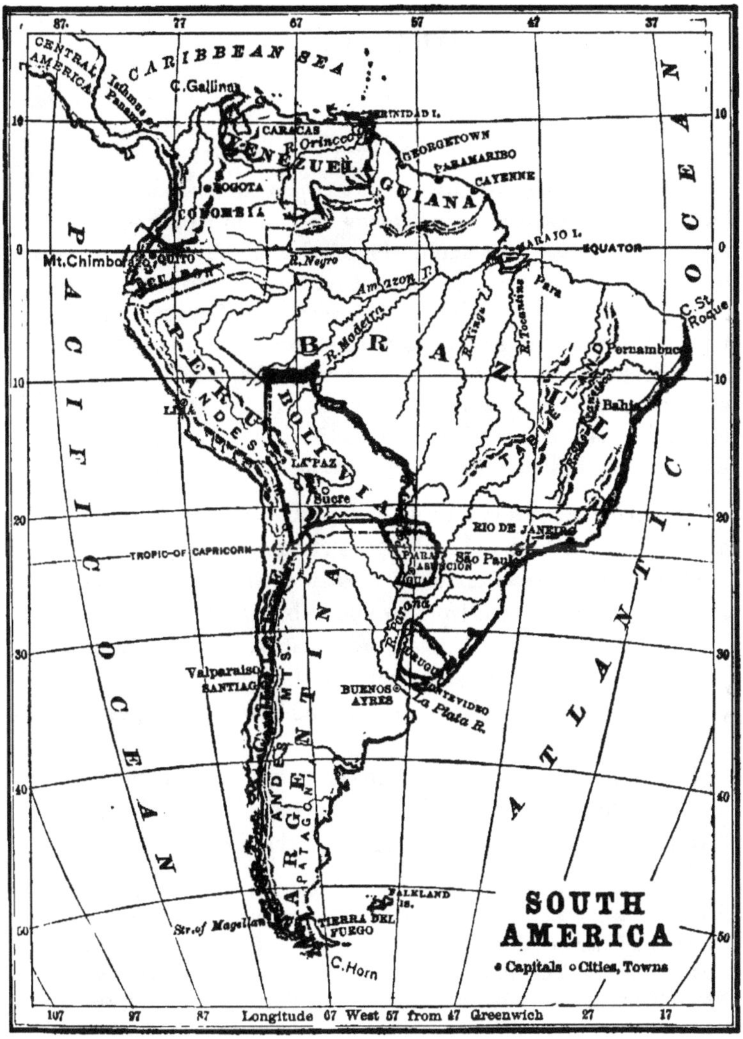

SOUTH AMERICA
• Capitals ∘ Cities, Towns
CARIBBEAN SEA
CENTRAL AMERICA
Isthmus of Panama
C. Gallinas
CARACAS
VENEZUELA
R. Orinoco
GEORGETOWN
PARAMARIBO
CAYENNE
GUIANA
BOGOTA
COLOMBIA
Mt. Chimborazo
QUITO
ECUADOR
EQUATOR
R. Negro
Amazon R.
R. Madeira
R. Xingu
R. Tocantins
Para
C. St. Roque
Pernambuco
Bahia
BRAZIL
PERU
ANDES
BOLIVIA
LA PAZ
Sucre
RIO DE JANEIRO
São Paulo
TROPIC OF CAPRICORN
PARAGUAY
ASUNCION
R. Parana
URUGUAY
MONTEVIDEO
La Plata R.
BUENOS AYRES
Valparaiso
SANTIAGO
ARGENTINA
PATAGONIA
FALKLAND IS.
TIERRA DEL FUEGO
Str. of Magellan
C. Horn
PACIFIC OCEAN
ATLANTIC OCEAN
Longitude 67 West 57 from 47 Greenwich

EUROPE.

L.—THE CONTINENT.

EUROPE lies east of the Atlantic, opposite the northern half of North America. It extends only about as far south as Cape Hatteras. One would suppose that the climate would be like that of the regions opposite on the American coast; but a large part is really very much warmer. Europe is the smallest of the continents, except Australia; and has a coast more broken than any of the others. The whole southwestern part is like a great peninsula, lying between the Mediterranean Sea and the Atlantic. The countries of Europe are all monarchies except *France* and *Switzerland.*

Eastern Europe is a great low plain, with mountains only on its borders. The longest river is the Volga.

Western Europe consists mostly of mountain lands and valleys, with small plains and table-lands.

The Alps are the **highest mountains.** The loftiest peak, Mont Blanc, is nearly three miles high.

The Danube, the Rhine, and the Rhone are the **principal rivers** of western Europe.

The **climate,** in all the coast countries, is much warmer than in coast regions opposite in America. Eastern Europe is cooler than western Europe.

EXERCISE.—(Open books to map of Europe, p. 267.) Name the oceans which border upon Europe; the seas and bays along the coast; a cluster of islands off the west coast; four islands in the Mediterranean. Find the mountains and rivers named in the lesson. Name the countries bordering upon the Mediterranean; **upon the**

Atlantic; the great country of eastern Europe; the small countries which touch the Black Sea; a little country between Italy and the German Empire. What (p. 210) is a republic?

LI.—THE BRITISH ISLES.
(PART I., PAGES 113-121.)

The British Isles together form the "United Kingdom of Great Britain and Ireland." The government has great possessions in America, Australia, Asia, and other parts of the world; and all these together form the *British Empire.* The British possessions are so scattered on all parts of the globe that people often say, "The sun never sets on the British flag," by which they mean, that there is never a time when it is not day in some country belonging to Great Britain.

Great Britain is but little larger than the State of Minnesota, yet it contains more than half as many people as the United States. England is the richest and most populous part.

Manufacturing and commerce are the **chief occupations,** but great care is given to agriculture. The leading manufactures are cotton, woolen, and linen goods, and articles made from iron and steel.

A Scotch Highlander.

England has more **great cities** than any other country of its size.

London is the capital of the British Empire, and is the largest city on the globe. It contains more than four millions of people.

Liverpool is the great seaport of northern England.

Manchester is the leading city of the world in cotton manufactures, and **Birmingham** in iron works.

Leeds is celebrated for its manufactures of wool.

Glasgow, in Scotland, is famous for the iron steamships built there; and **Edinburgh** for its university.

Dublin is the most important city in Ireland.

EXERCISE. — (Open books to map of British Isles.) Name the waters which separate Great Britain from the continent; Ireland from Great Britain. Name the different parts of Great Britain. Which includes the largest part of the island? Which has most of the great cities? Find all the cities named in the lesson. Read what is said in Part I. (pp. 116, 117) about London; about Manchester and Liverpool (p. 118); about Edinburgh (p. 120).

There are other large cities in England, about which you will like to learn at another time; and there are smaller ones which are very interesting. Find Cambridge; Oxford. At these two places are the old and celebrated English universities, of which we often hear. There is also a famous university in Ireland, at Dublin.

LII. — MAP LESSON.

Bound.   **Locate.**

ENGLAND. Strait of Dover, Lands End, Wales, Thames (*Temz*) River, LONDON, Liverpool, Manchester, Bir'-ming-ham, Leeds, Cambridge, Ox'-ford.

SCOTLAND. Heb'-ri-des Islands, Glas'-gow, Ed'-in-burgh.

IRELAND. Cape Clear, St. Georges Channel, Dublin, **Bel-fast'**, Cork.

BRITISH ISLES
Capitals
Cities, Towns
ORKNEY ISLANDS
C. Wrath
HEBRIDES ISLANDS
Moray Firth
Aberdeen
GRAMPIAN HILLS
Dundee
EDINBURGH
NORTH SEA
GREAT BRITAIN
SCOTLAND
ATLANTIC OCEAN
Malin Head
NORTH CHANNEL
Glasgow
Londonderry
Belfast
ISLE OF MAN
IRISH SEA
York
Leeds
Manchester
Sheffield
Galway
DUBLIN
ANGLESEY ID.
Liverpool
IRELAND
ENGLAND
WALES
Birmingham
ST. GEORGES CHANNEL
Cork
Queenstown
C. Clear
Thames R.
Oxford
Bristol
LONDON
Dover
Southampton
Str. of Dover
ATLANTIC OCEAN
Portsmouth
ISLE OF WIGHT
Lands End
Plymouth
ENGLISH CHANNEL
FRANCE
Longitude East from Greenwich
8
4
0
56
52

LIII.—FRANCE, BELGIUM, AND THE NETHERLANDS.

(Part I., Pages 122-133.)

These are among the most famous countries of Europe, on account of the great number of people they contain, their careful farming, and the immense variety of rich and costly things they manufacture. Belgium contains more persons to each square mile of territory than any other country in Europe. *France is the only great republic in Europe.*

France, Belgium, and the **Netherlands** lie on the coast of Europe, opposite England.

The chief **pursuits** of the people are agriculture, manufacturing, and commerce.

Among their **manufactures** are velvets, silks, ribbons, laces, gloves, jewelry, elegant cloths, carpets, furniture, and parlor ornaments.

Paris is the capital of France, and is the largest city on the continent of Europe.

Marseilles is the principal seaport, and **Lyons** is celebrated for its silk manufactures.

A Shepherd of the Landes.

Brussels, the capital of Belgium, is famous for its laces and carpets.

Amsterdam, in the Netherlands, has a very extensive commerce.

EXERCISE. — (Open books to map of Europe, p. 267.) Find the countries named. Bound each. Find Paris. What have you read (p. 126) about it? Turn to the map of Central Europe (p. 263). Find Mont Blanc; Lyons; Marseilles. What have you read (pp. 128, 129) about these cities? Find Brussels; Amsterdam. Many of the merchant ships that come to Amsterdam are laden with spices, coffee, medicines, choice woods, and other things from far-off lands in the Indies, belonging to the Netherlands.

Which of these three countries is a republic? In the southwestern part of France is a plain called the Landes, where the people are shepherds. They walk on stilts, and have raised seats so as to be able to overlook their flocks. The picture on the opposite page shows you one of the shepherds, resting on the high seat, and knitting.

LIV.—THE NORTH COUNTRIES.
(PART I., PAGES 133, 134.)

In the old times these north countries were famous for the courage and daring of the people, and their skill as sailors. The leaders were often called *sea kings*. They used to set out with their followers, and make voyages along the coast; and when they found an inviting region they would attack and often conquer it. Thus they gained possession of parts of England and France, and other territories much richer than their own. Some of these rovers discovered Iceland and Greenland, which still belong to Denmark; and it is said they even sailed as far as the New England coast, long before the time of Columbus.

Denmark, Sweden, and **Norway** lie on the coast farther north than the Netherlands. All taken together are often called the Scandinavian countries.

Norway and the western part of **Sweden** are high,

mountainous lands, famous for their **forests of tall pines** and firs, and their iron and copper ores.

Denmark is a low country. The islands are the best parts of it.

In Norway and Sweden many people are employed in the fisheries, the forests, and the mines; but in Denmark the principal **occupation** is farming.

The only **large cities** of the Scandinavian countries **are** their capitals.

Copenhagen, the **capital of Denmark,** is the largest and most celebrated of all the Scandinavian cities.

Stockholm, the capital of Sweden, is a beautiful city, situated on a cluster of islands.

In Stockholm.

EXERCISE. (Open books to map of Central Europe.) Find Denmark. Where are the islands? Find the capital. How is it situated? Turn to the map of Europe. Find Sweden and Norway. Find the capital of Sweden. These two countries are separate monarchies, each having its own king. Find the capital of Norway. What parallel near these two cities? Find where this parallel crosses North America. What sort of country is that part of North America?

LV.—REVIEW.

L. Where is Europe? How far south does it extend? What is remarkable about its size? Its coast? Describe eastern Europe; western Europe. What are the highest mountains in Europe? What, and how high, is the loftiest peak? Name the chief rivers of western Europe. Describe the climate of Europe.

LI. Where are the British Isles? Name the two great islands. What kingdom do they form? What is the British Empire? How large is Great Britain? How populous? What part of the island is most important? What are the leading kinds of business? The principal manufactures? Name the great cities. Which are in England? Which in Scotland? What important city in Ireland?

LIII. Where are France, Belgium, and the Netherlands? What are the chief pursuits of the people? Name some of the important manufactures. Name the largest cities of France; an important city in Belgium; in the Netherlands. What do you know about each of these cities? What distant possessions has the Netherlands? What is the government of France?

LIV. What and where are the Scandinavian countries? Describe Norway and Sweden; Denmark. What important pursuits in these countries? What are the largest Scandinavian cities? What important city in Norway? Write what you know about the country in France.

LVI.—THE SUNNY LANDS.
(Part I., Pages 135-145, 155-157.)

Three large peninsulas of Europe border upon the Mediterranean, and are famous for their fine climate, and their clear, sunny skies. Though no farther south than the middle of the United States, their climate and many important productions are more like those of Florida and Texas than Virginia and Kentucky. The eastern and middle peninsulas contained the first civilized nations in Europe, — the Greeks and Romans; and many things still remain there which show the wealth and grandeur of those ancient states.

The **peninsulas** of southern Europe contain Spain and Portugal, Italy, Greece, and European Turkey.

The **surface** in many parts is mountainous; but these countries have some of the most fertile valleys and small plains in Europe.

Eruption of Vesuvius.

The **climate** is delightful, with only short, mild winters.

Agriculture is the **main business**. Fruits, wine, and olive oil are the most abundant **productions**.

Italy and Spain contain a number of **great cities**. The largest are Naples, Rome, and Milan, in Italy, and Madrid, the capital of Spain. Rome, the most famous city of ancient times, is the capital of Italy.

SWITZERLAND AND GERMANY. 259

Constantinople is the capital and largest city of Turkey; **Lisbon,** of Portugal; and **Athens,** of Greece. **Venice** is an old city, built on a cluster of islands.

Exercise.— (Open books to the map of Europe.) Bound the countries named. What parallel crosses these countries? Find what States of our country are crossed by this parallel. The peninsulas of southern Europe all have high mountains along the northern border, shutting off the cold north winds. Besides, they are near the hot countries of Africa, with nothing to interrupt the warm south winds. That is one reason why they are so much warmer than the middle of our country. Find the cities named. (Milan is on the map of Central Europe.) In what country is each? Read what is said in Part I. about Madrid (p. 138), Rome (142), Venice (143), Naples (144), Constantinople and Athens (157).

A Spanish Peasant.

LVII.—SWITZERLAND AND GERMANY.
(Part I., Pages 145-153.)

The great kingdom of Prussia, the smaller kingdoms of Saxony, Bavaria, and Wurtemburg, and a number of other little states in the middle part of Europe, are all peopled by Germans. In 1871 these states united, forming the *Empire of Germany,* and made *King William of Prussia* their emperor. Germany is celebrated for its schools and its learned men, and for the treasures of painting and sculpture, and other interesting things, collected in the cities.

Switzerland is a small republic, situated among the highest mountain lands of Europe. Geneva is its most important city. Bern is its capital.

The kingdom of Prussia and a number of smaller states, together form the **Empire of Germany.**

The **surface** of southern Germany is mountainous,

Dresden Market.

but the northern part is a plain. The Rhine, which flows through the highlands, is the most famous **river.**

The **climate** is cooler than on the coast farther west.

Farming, wool growing, and manufacturing are the leading **occupations** of the Germans.

The **largest cities** are Berlin, Hamburg, and Breslau. Munich, Dresden, and Leipzig are also noted.

Berlin, the capital of Prussia, is also the capital of the empire.

Exercise. — (Open books to map of Central Europe.) Find Switzerland. What famous mountain just outside of it? Find Geneva. Find Bern. Bound the German Empire. Find Berlin. Find Munich.

Find Hamburg. Find Breslau. Find Dresden and Leipzig.

LVIII. — AUSTRIA-HUNGARY.

(Part I., Pages 154, 155.)

The leading state of this great empire is *Austria*, situated in the western highlands south of the Danube. The Austrians and their near neighbors are Germans. The other peoples of the empire speak different languages, and are very unlike the Austrians. The kingdom of *Hungary*, in the middle part, is the largest division of the empire.

Austria-Hungary lies in central Europe, southeast of the German Empire. It consists of Austria, Hungary, and a number of

Street Scene in Austria.

provinces, united under an Austrian emperor.

The **surface** of Hungary is composed largely of plains.

The other parts of the empire are generally hilly or mountainous. The Danube is the greatest **river**.

The **climate** is warmer than that of Germany.

The **chief pursuit** is agriculture, but manufacturing and mining are also important. Grain, flax, and wine are produced in the rich plains.

The **greatest cities** are Vienna, Budapest, and Prague. **Vienna** is the capital of the empire.

EXERCISE. — (Open books to map of Europe.) Bound Austria-Hungary; find its capital. What have you read (p. 154) about Vienna? Turn to the map of Central Europe, and find another capital in this empire; this is the capital of Hungary. The Danube flows through it: and, formerly, the parts on the opposite sides of the river were separate cities, named Pesth and Buda; but now they are united into one, and its name is Budapest.

Find Prague. In what province is it? Bohemia was once a kingdom, and Prague was its capital. Find a city directly east of Prague. There are famous salt mines near Cracow. In the mountains between Cracow and Vienna, are the most productive gold and silver mines in Europe. What parts of Italy and France are shown in this map? Where will you find the rest? (On map of Europe.)

LIX.—MAP LESSON.

Bound.	Locate.
GERMAN EMPIRE.	Rhine River, BER′-LIN, Bres′-lau, Hamburg, DRES′-DEN, Leip′-zig, MUNICH.
AUSTRIA-HUNGARY.	Alps Mountains, Danube River, VIENNA, BU′-DA-PEST, Prague.
SWITZERLAND.	Alps Mountains, Geneva, BERN.
THE NETHERLANDS.	Rhine River, THE HAGUE (*Hāg*), Amsterdam.
BELGIUM.	BRUS′SELS.
DENMARK.	CO-PEN-HA′-GEN.
ITALY.	Alps Mountains, Po River, Mi-lan′, Venice.
FRANCE.	Mont Blanc, Rhone River, Lyons.

CENTRAL EUROPE
• Capitals ○ Cities, Towns
NORTH SEA
SWEDEN
DENMARK
COPENHAGEN
BALTIC SEA
BORNHOLM I.
Skager Rack
Cattegat
Danzig
Hamburg
Bremen
Amsterdam
THE HAGUE
Rotterdam
Hanover
BERLIN
Warsaw
GERMAN EMPIRE
PRUSSIA
RUSSIA
Leipzig
DRESDEN
Breslau
Cologne
Frankfurt-am-Main
Prague
BOHEMIA
Brunn
Cracow
PARIS
Metz
BAVARIA
AUSTRIA-HUNGARY
MUNICH
VIENNA
BUDAPEST
Zurich
BERN
Geneva
Lyons
Mt. Blanc
Milan
Venice
Trieste
Turin
Po R.
ITALY
BOSNIA
ADRIATIC SEA
Marseilles
Gulf of Genoa
Florence
Gulf of The Lion
MEDITERRANEAN SEA
ROME
Ragusa
Longitude East 10 from Greenwich 15

LX.—RUSSIA AND ROUMANIA.
(Part I., Pages 158, 159.)

Russia and the little kingdom of Roumania lie in the great plain of eastern Europe. We have already noticed the frozen lands on the Arctic shores, the vast country south of them, and the smaller forests among cultivated lands that fill the middle portion of Russia. In the south, west of the

A Friendly Chat.

river Don, are rich prairies, almost like those of the Mississippi. Towards the Caspian, the land is poor, and the best parts are only pasture grounds. In some respects they are much like the pampas of South America. The Cossacks, who live there, raise herds of horses and cattle, and are about as daring riders as the Gauchos (p. 106).

Russia fills nearly all the great plain of eastern Europe. The northern part is very cold, and is mostly a forest region.

The **settled portions** of Russia are principally in the middle and southwestern parts, where the climate is moderate, and there are rich farming lands.

The **great business** of the people is farming and stock raising. Fine crops of wheat and flax, and large herds of horses and cattle, are raised.

The **largest cities** are St. Petersburg and Moscow. **St. Petersburg** is the capital.

Roumania is a small kingdom in the plains at the mouth of the Danube. It contains rich wheat lands, and is a farming country. Bucharest is its capital.

EXERCISE.—(Open books to the map of Europe.) Bound Russia. Find St. Petersburg: what have you read (p. 159) about it? Find Moscow. This was the capital before St. Petersburg was built. The Russians are a sociable people, fond of meeting and chatting together. The picture shows a little group who seem to be having a fine time. One of them, you see, is a wandering musician, with his instrument on his shoulders, and a staff in his hand. I wonder what *sort* of music he can make?

Find Roumania. What countries are its neighbors? To what country (p. 155) did Roumania and the little states south of the Danube once belong?

LXI.—REVIEW.

LVI. What countries of Europe are in the southern peninsulas? Describe their surface; their climate; the chief occupations and productions. Name the largest cities of the southern countries. Name the capital of each of these countries.

LVII. What and where is Switzerland? Its most important city? What do you know about Geneva? What is the capital of

Switzerland? What forms the Empire of Germany? Describe the surface. Name the chief river. Describe the climate. What is the chief pursuit of the people? Name the three principal cities. What three others are interesting? What makes them so? What is the capital of the German Empire?

LVIII. Where is Austria-Hungary? Of what does it consist? What is the surface? The climate? The chief pursuit of the people? Name some of the chief crops; the three largest cities. What is the capital of the empire?

LX. What countries lie in the plains of eastern Europe? Where is Russia? What are the most settled portions? Why are these better to live in than the northern? What is the chief pursuit? What do the farms produce? Name the two chief cities. Tell something about each. What and where is Roumania?

LXII.—MAP LESSON.

Bound.

Russia. Austria-Hungary. Italy.
Sweden. Rou-ma'-ni-a (*Roo-*). Spain.
Norway. Turkey. Portugal.
German Empire. Greece. France.

Locate.

Switzerland. Alps Mountains. Constantinople.
Denmark. Pyrenees. Athens.
British Isles. U'-ral. St. Pe'-ters-burg.
Cor'-si-ca. Cau'-ca-sus. Mos'-cow.
Sar-din'-i-a. Volga River. Naples.
Sic'-i-ly. Rhine River. Rome.
Black Sea. Rhone River. Marseilles.
Cas'-pi-an Sea. Danube River. Madrid.
Bal'-tic Sea (*Ball-*). London. Lisbon.
North Sea. Paris. Stock'-holm.
Ad-ri-at'-ic Sea. Berlin. Chris-ti-a'-ni-a.
Gib-ral'-tar Strait. Vienna. Bu-cha-rest'.

EUROPE
● Capitals ○ Cities, Towns
ARCTIC OCEAN
North Cape
ARCTIC CIRCLE
ICELAND
ATLANTIC OCEAN
BRITISH ISLES
IRELAND
SCOTLAND
ENGLAND
LONDON
NORTH SEA
DENMARK
STOCKHOLM
CHRISTIANIA
BALTIC SEA
Gulf of Bothnia
White Sea
Dwina R.
L. Onega
L. Ladoga
ST. PETERSBURG
Moscow
RUSSIA
Ural R.
Volga R.
URAL MOUNTAINS
Dnieper R.
Don R.
Warsaw
Odessa
GERMAN EMPIRE
BERLIN
Elbe R.
AUSTRIA
VIENNA
HUNGARY
ROUMANIA
BULGARIA
Adrianople
CONSTANTINOPLE
TURKEY
Salonika
BLACK SEA
CAUCASUS MTS.
CASPIAN SEA
ASIA
BAY OF BISCAY
Bordeaux
PARIS
Seine R.
Lyons
Rhone R.
Marseilles
C. Finisterre
LISBON
PORTUGAL
MADRID
SPAIN
PYRENEES
Barcelona
CORSICA
SARDINIA
ROME
Naples
APENNINES
Adriatic Sea
Venice
ITALY
SICILY
Messina
Strait of Gibraltar
MEDITERRANEAN SEA
AFRICA
Cyprus
Long. West
Longitude
East
from Greenwich

AFRICA.

LXIII.—NORTHERN AFRICA.
(Part I., Pages 160-164.)

Africa is the largest continent, except Asia; but it contains neither great arms of the sea nor peninsulas, and has no vast systems of high mountains. In the northern part, there is a great rainless region; but in the middle, are some of the largest fresh-water lakes and rivers in the world.

Camel Drivers.

Northern Africa includes the Sahara, Egypt, and the Barbary States. The native inhabitants are whites.

The **Sahara** is a rainless region, but contains many fertile *oases*. *Fezzan* is a group of the largest ones.

Egypt is the most important country in Africa. The Nile valley has always been famous for its abundant crops, and it was once the great grain field of the world. **Cairo** is the capital. The **Barbary** States are the fertile countries north of the Sahara. Algeria belongs to France.

EXERCISE. — (Open books to map of Africa.) Find the Atlas Mountains; the Isthmus of Suez. A ship canal crosses this isthmus; what waters does it connect? Find the Barbary States; Egypt; their capitals. Algeria used to belong to Turkey, and the governor was called the "*Dey of Algiers.*" What (p. 160) are the oases? Find Fezzan.

Algerian Girl.

LXIV.—MIDDLE AND SOUTHERN AFRICA.
(PART I., PAGES 165, 166.)

In middle Africa, are wonderful forests, vast treeless plains, and immense marshes, with many of the largest animals in the world. Many of the trees and smaller plants yield food for the savage tribes; and a great number furnish gums, oils, and other valuable articles. The plumes of the ostrich and the ivory tusks of the elephant are also of great value.

Middle Africa is the land of the negroes, and most of the tribes are savages. There are a very few white men, at trading posts or mission stations.

Southern Africa contains many British and Dutch colonists.

Cape Colony is the most important British possession in Africa. It has fertile lands on the coast, fine pasture grounds farther inland, and rich diamond fields and gold mines near the northern border. It exports wine and wool as well as gold and diamonds. Cape Town is the capital.

Zulus.

Exercise.—(Open books to map of Africa.) Find Cape Colony; Cape Town; four large rivers in Africa; two large lakes.

LXV.—MAP LESSON.

Bound.		Locate.	
Egypt.	Cape Good Hope.	Gulf of Guinea.	Kongo River.
Algeria.	Isthmus of Suez.	Atlas Mountains.	Cairo.
Morocco.	Madagascar.	Lake Victoria Nyanza.	Algiers.
Tripoli.	Mediterranean Sea.	Nile River.	Cape Town.
Cape Colony.	Red Sea.	Niger River.	Fez.

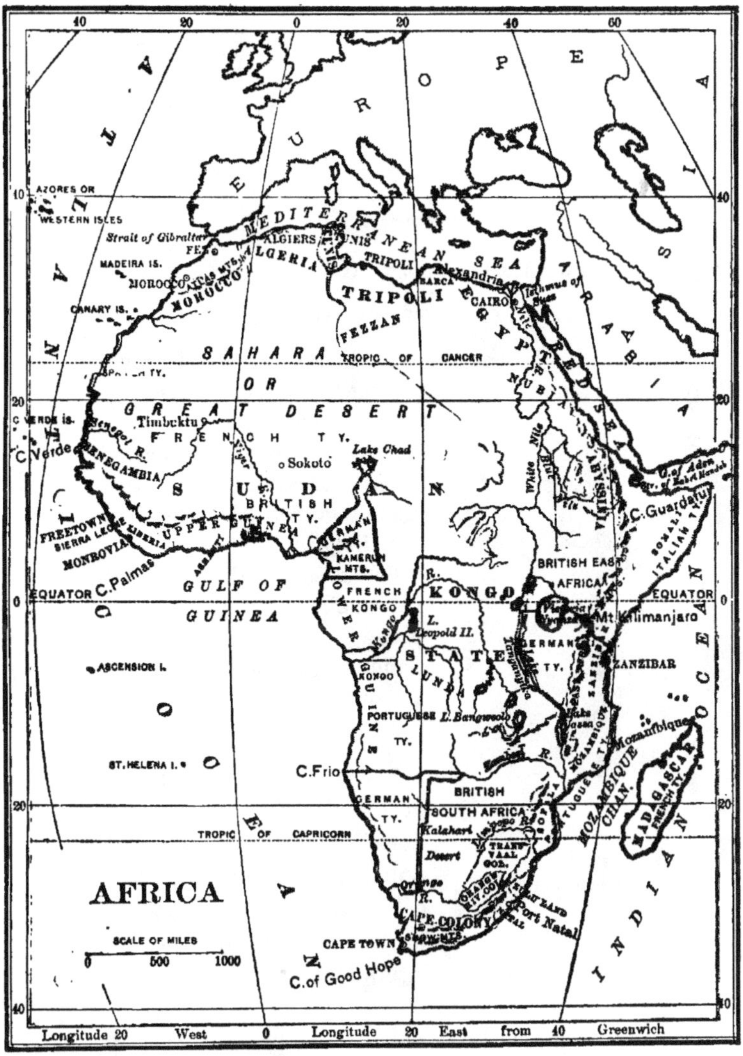
AFRICA
SCALE OF MILES
0 500 1000
EUROPE
ASIA
ARABIA
ATLANTIC OCEAN
INDIAN OCEAN
AZORES OR WESTERN ISLES
Strait of Gibraltar
MADEIRA IS.
CANARY IS.
C. VERDE IS.
C. Verde
MEDITERRANEAN SEA
ALGIERS
TUNIS
ALGERIA
TRIPOLI
MOROCCO
FEZZAN
Alexandria
CAIRO
EGYPT
RED SEA
SAHARA OR GREAT DESERT
TROPIC OF CANCER
Timbuktu
FRENCH TY.
SENEGAMBIA
Sokoto
Lake Chad
SUDAN
BRITISH TY.
FREETOWN
SIERRA LEONE
LIBERIA
MONROVIA
UPPER GUINEA
C. Palmas
GULF OF GUINEA
EQUATOR
KAMERUN MTS.
FRENCH KONGO
KONGO STATE
L. Leopold II.
ABYSSINIA
White Nile
G. of Aden
C. Guardafui
ITALIAN TY.
BRITISH EAST AFRICA
Mt. Kilimanjaro
GERMAN TY.
ZANZIBAR
ASCENSION I.
ST. HELENA I.
PORTUGUESE TY.
L. Bangweolo
Mozambique
MOZAMBIQUE CHAN.
MADAGASCAR
FRENCH TY.
C. Frio
GERMAN TY.
BRITISH SOUTH AFRICA
Kalahari Desert
TRANSVAAL
TROPIC OF CAPRICORN
Orange R.
CAPE COLONY
Port Natal
CAPE TOWN
C. of Good Hope
Longitude 20 West 0 Longitude 20 East from 40 Greenwich

ASIA.

LXVI.—NORTHERN AND WESTERN ASIA.
(PART I., PAGES 167-170, AND 179.)

THE Russians, who possess the whole of eastern Europe, rule over all of northern Asia. The northernmost portion is called *Siberia,* and the southwestern, *Russian Turkestan.* These possessions and Russia itself together form the *Russian Empire.*

Southeast of the Aral Sea are small independent countries. Their people are mostly wandering herdsmen, but there are cultivated lands and cities in the best parts.

Northern Asia forms part of the Russian Empire, but does not contain a large population. *Siberia* is very cold, except in the southern part. *Turkestan* has hot summers, but very cold winters; and a large part is quite dry.

There are **rich lands** in the eastern part of Russian Turkestan, and also in the southern part of Siberia.

Persian Water Carrier.

Turkey, Persia, and **Arabia** contain vast dry regions, with only wandering herdsmen for inhabitants; but they have, also, some of the most fertile lands in Asia.

All of these three countries **produce** fruits, drugs, and perfumeries; and Arabia yields coffee and spices.

Turkey is part of the Turkish Empire, with its capital at Constantinople, in Europe.

Persia is a kingdom, and Teheran is its capital.

EXERCISE.— (Open books to the map of Asia.) Find Siberia. Find Russian Turkestan; a body of water within it. Find Persia; Turkey; Arabia. What interesting places in Turkey (pp. 167, 168) did you read about? Find Ispahan; what have you read (p. 170) about it?

LXVII.—THE INDIES.

(PART I., PAGES 171, 172.)

We have already seen what a wonderful region this part of Asia is. Long ago, when the sea-going peoples of Europe were each trying to gain as much as possible of the wealth of the Indies, they began to establish trading stations on the coasts of the peninsulas and the islands. Little by little, and in various ways, they have increased their territories, until now the larger part of the Indies belongs to them. But part of the eastern peninsula is still ruled by native peoples.

The **Indies include** two great peninsulas and a large group of islands at the southeast of Asia.

The **climate** is hot, with abundance of rain.

Rare woods, spices, ivory, and precious stones are part of the **natural wealth.** The **cultivated productions** are coffee, sugar, indigo, rice, cotton, and opium.

Great Britain controls nearly the whole of the western peninsula, as well as the island of Ceylon and the west shore of the eastern peninsula. *Calcutta* is the capital of British India.

France has possession of a large part of the eastern peninsula.

The **United States** controls the Philippine Islands. **Manila** is the capital.

The **Netherlands** holds most of the other islands, excepting parts of Borneo and New Guinea. Batavia, in Java, is the capital of the Dutch Indies.

The northern part of Borneo is controlled by Great Britain.

A Hindu Cook.

Parts of New Guinea also belong to **Great Britain and to Germany**. The natives are black.

EXERCISE.— (Open books to the map of Asia.) Find **India**. What great river has it? What have you read (p. 172) about the plains of the Ganges? Find a city at the mouth of the Ganges. What do you know about it? Find Anam. Find the Philippine islands. Name four other large islands. Which islands are wholly south of the equator?

The native islanders are of the brown race. The **native people** on the plains of the Ganges are called *Hindus*. You know what skillful workmen they are

LXVIII.—THE EMPIRES OF CHINA AND JAPAN.
(Part I., Pages 173-178.)

The *Chinese Empire* is not nearly so large as the Russian Empire, but it contains about three times as many people. The rich plains along the rivers in *China* are the most populous part. The *Japanese Empire* consists of a cluster of islands, somewhat larger than the British Isles. They

A Chinese Wheelbarrow.

lie opposite our country. **The people of both empires belong** to the yellow race.

The **Chinese Empire** occupies the larger part of middle and eastern Asia. The capital is Peking.

The most famous **productions** are tea, silks, porcelain, and curious carvings in ivory and wood.

Tokyo is the capital of Japan. The **productions** are much like those of China.

The Japanese are more advanced in civilization than **any** other nation of their race.

276 GEOGRAPHICAL PRIMER.

Interior of a Japanese House.

EXERCISE. — (Open books to the map of Asia.) Find China; the Himalaya Mountains; Tibet; Mongolia. What have you read (pp. 176-178) about each? Find Peking; Canton. What have you read (p. 175) about these cities? about the peoples? Find the Japanese Islands; the name of the largest; an important city in Hondo.

LXIX. — MAP LESSON.

Bound.

TURKEY. INDIA.
PERSIA. CHINESE EMP.
ARABIA. JAPANESE EMP.

Locate.

Siberia. Al-tai′ Mts.
Turk-es-tan′(Rus.) Ar′-al Sea.
Phil′-ip-pine Isles. O′-bi River(-be).
Mo-luc′-ca Isles. Gan′-ges.
New Guinea. Yen-i-se′-i(-sa′).
Bor′-ne-o. Yang′-tze Kiang.
Su-ma′-tra(-mah′-). Ho-ang′ Ho.
Ja′-va (Jah′-). To-ky′-o.
Cey-lon′. Pe-king′.
Ben-gal′ B.(-gawl′). Can′-ton.
Himalaya Mts. Cal-cut′-ta.

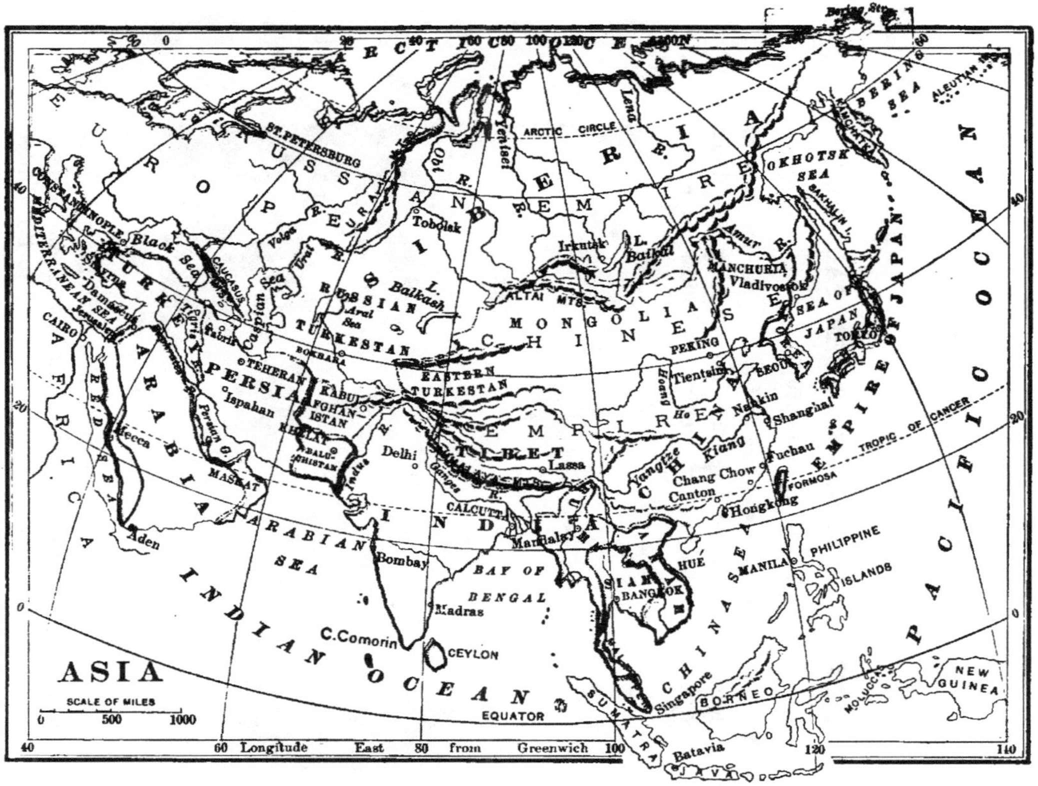
ASIA
SCALE OF MILES
0 500 1000
Longitude East from Greenwich
ARCTIC CIRCLE
TROPIC OF CANCER
EQUATOR
EUROPE
AFRICA
ARABIA
PERSIA
INDIA
TIBET
CHINESE EMPIRE
MONGOLIA
SIBERIA
RUSSIAN EMPIRE
RUSSIAN TURKESTAN
EASTERN TURKESTAN
AFGHANISTAN
BALUCHISTAN
MANCHURIA
EMPIRE OF JAPAN
PHILIPPINE ISLANDS
BORNEO
SUMATRA
JAVA
NEW GUINEA
CEYLON
PACIFIC OCEAN
INDIAN OCEAN
ARABIAN SEA
BAY OF BENGAL
CHINA SEA
SEA OF JAPAN
OKHOTSK SEA
BERING SEA
Bering Str.
MEDITERRANEAN SEA
RED SEA
Black Sea
Caspian Sea
Aral Sea
Persian G.
L. Balkash
L. Baikal
ST. PETERSBURG
CONSTANTINOPLE
CAIRO
Jerusalem
Damascus
Smyrna
Mecca
Aden
MASKAT
TEHERAN
Tabriz
Ispahan
KABUL
BOKHARA
Tobolsk
Irkutsk
Vladivostok
PEKING
Tientsin
SEOUL
TOKIO
Nankin
Shanghai
Fuchau
Chang Chow
Canton
Hongkong
FORMOSA
Lassa
Delhi
CALCUTTA
Bombay
Madras
C.Comorin
Mandalay
BANGKOK
HUE
MANILA
Singapore
Batavia
SAKHALIN
KAMCHATKA
CAUCASUS
ALTAI MTS.
Lena
Yenisei
Obi R.
Amur R.
Volga
Ural
Tigris
Indus
Ganges
Hoang Ho
Yangtze Kiang

AUSTRALIA.

LXX.—AUSTRALIA AND THE PACIFIC.
(PART I., PAGES 180-183.)

WE have noticed in the Pacific Ocean great numbers of small islands. They differ much in character, but if we study them we find there are only two kinds. Some are

Load of Wool in Australia.

groups of volcanoes with a strip of coast land around them. These are *volcanic* islands. The *Hawaiian Islands*, about midway between Mexico and China, belong to the United

States, and are the most famous of this class. Other islands are low and flat; some being only rings of land. These are *coral* islands; that is, the soil is formed, and the plants are growing, on the top of a bank of coral.

Australia, the smallest of the continents, belongs to Great Britain. The southeastern part is best known, and contains most of the white inhabitants.

Low mountains, rich in gold, border the coast; and rivers flow from them westward through fertile **plains.**

Wool growing, wheat raising, and gold mining are the **chief occupations** of the people. Cattle raising is important.

The **white inhabitants** are mostly from Great Britain. As yet they are fewer in number than the population of New York State. The natives are black.

EXERCISE. — (Open books to the map of eastern hemisphere.) Find Australia. On which side of the equator is it? What are some of the strange things (p. 181) one may see in Australia?

LXXI. — REVIEW.

LXIII. What countries are in northern Africa? Of what race are the native people? What is the Sahara? Egypt? Name the Barbary States. Which belongs to France?

LXIV. Who are the people of middle Africa? What useful things come from middle Africa? What white colonists are in South Africa? What does Cape Colony contain that is valuable?

LXVI. To what country does northern Asia belong? What three important countries in western Asia? What sort of countries are they? What do they produce? Of what empire is Turkey a part? What is its capital? What is Persia?

LXVII. What do the Indies include? What is the climate? What are the productions? What part of the Indies belongs to Great Britain? To France? To Netherlands? To United States?

LXVIII. Where is the Chinese Empire? What is the capital? What is the climate of China? What are the leading productions? What forms the Empire of Japan? What is its capital? Of what race are the Chinese and Japanese?

LXX. To whom does Australia belong? What part is best known? Describe that part. What are the pursuits of the white inhabitants? Where did they come from? How great is the number of them? Of what color are the natives?

LXXII.—EASTERN HEMISPHERE (Examination).

What kingdom do the British Isles form? Of what does the British Empire consist? What European countries border on the Atlantic? What is the government of France? What small republic in central Europe? What European countries border on the Mediterranean? What two empires in central Europe? What great country in eastern Europe? Where is the rest of the Russian Empire?

What high mountains in Europe? Name the highest peak in Europe. Name four important rivers in Europe. In what country is London? Paris? Berlin? Vienna? Constantinople? Naples? Liverpool? Glasgow? Manchester? Edinburgh? Lyons? Madrid? Lisbon? Marseilles? Dublin? Munich? Rome? Athens? St. Petersburg? Moscow? Milan? Bucharest?

What three important countries in western Asia? What great empire in middle and eastern Asia? Where is the Japanese Empire? What important articles come from China and Japan? Of what do the Indies consist? What European countries control the Indies? What valuable things come from the Indies? In what country is Peking? Tokyo? Canton? Calcutta?

What countries are in northern Africa? Where is Cairo? Algiers? What race occupies middle Africa? What valuable things come from middle Africa? What is the principal country in South Africa? What precious things come from there? What important town in South Africa? To what country does Australia belong? What does it produce?

TABLES.

POPULATION OF THE PRINCIPAL CITIES IN THE WORLD.

UNITED STATES.

New England.

Portland, Me.,	50,000
Manchester, N.H.,	57,000
Boston, Mass.,	561,000
Worcester, Mass.,	119,000
Fall River, Mass.,	105,000
Lynn, Mass.,	69,000
New Bedford, Mass.,	63,000
Lawrence, Mass.,	63,000
Lowell, Mass.,	95,000
Cambridge, Mass.,	92,000
Somerville, Mass.,	62,000
Springfield, Mass.,	62,000
Providence, R.I.,	176,000
New Haven, Conn.,	108,000
Hartford, Conn.,	80,000

Middle States.

New York, N.Y.,	3,500,000
Buffalo, N.Y.,	353,000
Rochester, N.Y.,	163,000
Syracuse, N.Y.,	108,000
Albany, N.Y.,	94,000
Troy, N.Y.,	61,000
Newark, N.J.,	246,000
Jersey City, N.J.,	207,000
Paterson, N.J.,	105,000
Camden, N.J.,	76,000
Trenton, N.J.,	73,000
Hoboken, N.J.,	59,000
Philadelphia, Pa.,	1,294,000
Pittsburg, Pa.,	322,000
Allegheny, Pa.,	128,000
Scranton, Pa.,	102,000
Reading, Pa.,	79,000
Wilmington, Del.,	77,000
Baltimore, Md.,	509,000
Washington, D.C.,	279,000
Richmond, Va.,	85,000
Wheeling, W. Va.,	39,000

Southern States.

Wilmington, N.C.,	21,000
Charleston, S.C.,	56,000
Atlanta, Ga.,	90,000
Jacksonville, Fla.,	28,000
Mobile, Ala.,	39,000
New Orleans, La.,	287,000
Memphis, Tenn.,	102,000
Nashville, Tenn.,	81,000
Little Rock, Ark.,	38,000
San Antonio, Tex.,	53,000

Central States.

Louisville, Ky.,	205,000
Cleveland, O.,	382,000
Cincinnati, O.,	326,000
Columbus, O.,	126,000
Toledo, O.,	132,000
Dayton, O.,	85,000
Indianapolis, Ind.,	169,000
Evansville, Ind.,	59,000
Chicago, Ill.,	1,700,000
Detroit, Mich.,	286,000
Grand Rapids, Mich.,	88,000
Milwaukee, Wis.,	285,000
Minneapolis, Minn.,	203,000
St. Paul, Minn.,	163,000
Duluth, Minn.,	53,000
Des Moines, Ia.,	62,000
St. Louis, Mo.,	575,000
Kansas City, Mo.,	164,000
St. Joseph, Mo.,	103,000
Kansas City, Kas.,	52,000
Omaha, Neb.,	103,000
Lincoln, Neb.,	40,000

Pacific States.

Denver, Col.,	134,000
Salt Lake City, Utah,	54,000
Seattle, Wash,	81,000
Portland, Ore.,	91,000
San Francisco, Cal.,	343,000
Los Angeles, Cal.,	103,000

DOMINION OF CANADA.

Montreal, P.Q.,	268,000
Toronto, Ont.,	208,000
Quebec, P.Q.,	69,000
Hamilton, Ont.,	53,000
Ottawa, Ont.,	60,000
St. John, N.B.,	41,000
Halifax, N.S.,	41,000

MEXICO, CENTRAL AMERICA, AND WEST INDIES.

Mexico, Mex.,	345,000
Puebla, Mex.,	94,000
Guadalajara, Mex.,	101,000
Guatemala, C.A.,	97,000
Havana, Cuba,	282,000
San Juan P'to Rico,	32,000

SOUTH AMERICA.

Rio de Janeiro, Brazil,	750,000
Bahia, Brazil,	230,000
Pernambuco, Brazil,	120,000
São Paulo, Brazil,	332,000
Para, Brazil,	100,000
Buenos Ayres, Argentina,	1,026,000
Montevideo, Uruguay,	309,000
Asuncion, Paraguay,	60,000
Caracas, Venezuela,	78,000
Santiago, Chile,	378,000
Valparaiso, Chile,	175,000
La Paz, Bolivia,	67,000
Lima, Peru,	130,000
Quito, Ecuador,	80,000
Bogota, Colombia,	120,000

EUROPE.

London, Eng.,	4,600,000
Liverpool, Eng.,	685,000
Manchester, Eng.,	544,000
Birmingham, Eng.,	522,000
Leeds, Eng.,	429,000
Sheffield, Eng.,	381,000
Bristol, Eng.,	329,000
Glasgow, Scot.,	786,000
Edinburgh, Scot.,	317,000
Belfast, Ire.,	349,000
Dublin, Ire.,	291,000
Paris, France,	2,763,000
Lyons, France,	472,000
Marseilles, France,	518,000
Bordeaux, France,	252,000
Lille, France,	206,000
Antwerp, Belgium,	292,000
Brussels, Belgium,	599,000
Amsterdam, Neth.,	551,000
Rotterdam, Neth.,	370,000
Copenhagen, Den.,	378,000
Stockholm, Swed.,	301,000
Christiania, Nor.,	228,000
Berlin, Ger.,	2,040,000

Hamburg, Ger.,	803,000	Florence, Italy,	206,000	Bangkok, Siam,	400,000
Munich, Ger.,	588,000	Palermo, Sicily,	310,000	Canton, China,	2,900,000
Dresden, Ger.,	514,000	Athens, Greece,	112,000	Peking, China,	1,000,000
Leipzig, Ger.,	503,000	Constantinople, Turkey,	1,125,000	Fuchau, China,	624,000
Breslau, Ger.,	417,000			Tientsin, China,	750,000
Cologne, Ger.,	429,000	Salonika, Turkey,	105,000	Shanghai, China,	651,000
Vienna, Aust.-Hung.,	1,675,000	Adrianople, Turkey,	71,000	Tokyo, Japan,	1,819,000
		St. Petersburg, Russia,	1,267,000		
Budapest, Aust.-Hung.,	732,000	Moscow, Russia,	989,000	**AFRICA.**	
Prague, Aust.-Hung.,	202,000	Warsaw, Russia,	638,000	Cairo, Egypt,	570,000
		Odessa, Russia,	405,000	Alexandria, Egypt,	320,000
Bucharest, Rou.,	282,000			Tunis, Tunis,	250,000
Zurich, Switz.,	153,000	**ASIA.**		Algiers, Algeria,	97,000
Geneva, Switz.,	105,000			Cape Town, Cape Col.	78,000
Madrid, Spain,	540,000	Smyrna, Turkey,	201,000		
Barcelona, Spain,	533,000	Damascus, Turkey,	225,000		
Lisbon, Port.,	357,000	Tabriz, Persia,	200,000		
Naples, Italy,	564,000	Teheran, Persia,	280,000	**AUSTRALIA, ETC.**	
Rome, Italy,	463,000	Mecca, Arabia,	60,000	Melbourne, Aus.,	496,000
Milan, Italy,	492,000	Calcutta, Br. India,	1,127,000	Sydney, Australia,	482,000
Turin, Italy,	336,000	Bombay, Br. India,	776,000	Manila, Phil. Is.,	220,000
Genoa, Italy,	235,000	Madras, Br. India,	509,000	Honolulu, Haw. Is.,	39,000

LENGTHS OF THE PRINCIPAL RIVERS OF THE WORLD.

NEW WORLD.	Miles.	OLD WORLD.	Miles.
Mississippi-Missouri, North Amer.	4,200	Nile, Africa	3,900
Amazon, South America	3,400	Yangtze Kiang, Asia	3,200
La Plata, South America	2,500	Yenisei, Asia	3,000
Mackenzie, North America	2,100	Obi, Asia	3,000
St. Lawrence, North America	2,100	Niger, Africa	2,900
Yukon, North America	2,000	Hoang Ho, Asia	2,800
Saskatchewan, North America	1,900	Lena, Asia	2,800
Rio Grande, North America	1,800	Kongo, Africa	2,800
São Francisco, South America	1,800	Amur, Asia	2,700
Arkansas, North America	1,500	Volga, Europe	2,300
Orinoco, South America	1,500	Euphrates, Asia	2,000
Columbia, North America	1,400	Indus, Asia	1,900
Ohio-Alleghany, North America	1,300	Ganges, Asia	1,800
Red, North America	1,200	Brahmaputra, Asia	1,800
Colorado, North America	1,000	Zambezi, Africa	1,600
Susquehanna, North America	400	Danube, Europe	1,600
Connecticut, North America	400	Orange, Africa	1,200
Hudson, North America	300	Rhine, Europe	900

HEIGHT OF MOUNTAINS.

NEW WORLD.	Feet.	OLD WORLD.	Feet.
Aconcagua, Chile	23,082	Mount Everest (Himalaya)	29,002
Sorata, Bolivia	21,286	Mount Dapsang, Tibet	28,278
Chimborazo, Ecuador	20,517	Mount Kanchinjinga (Himal.)	28,156
McKinley, Alaska	20,464	Dhaulagiri (Himal.)	26,826
Orizaba, Mexico	18,314	Kilimanjaro, Africa	20,000
St. Elias, Alaska	18,024	Elbruz (Caucasus)	18,846
Popocatepetl, Mexico	17,784	Hindu Kush, Afghanistan	18,000
Mount Whitney, California	14,502	Ararat, Armenia	17,130
Longs Peak, Colorado	14,271	Mont Blanc (Alps)	15,744
Pikes Peak, Colorado	14,111	Monte Rosa (Alps)	15,208